THE WIDOWER
CONSIDERS CANDLES

THE WIDOWER
CONSIDERS CANDLES

❄

Robert Lavett Smith

FCP

Full Court Press
Englewood Cliffs, New Jersey

First Edition

Copyright © 2014 by Robert Lavett Smith

Published in the United States of America
by Full Court Press, 601 Palisade Avenue
Englewood Cliffs, NJ 07632
fullcourtpressnj.com

ISBN 978-1-938812-38-5
Library of Congress Control No. 2014952111

Book Design by Barry Sheinkopf for Bookshapers
(bookshapers.com)

Author Photo by Laurie Sato

FCP Colophon by Liz Sedlack

Cover art courtesy istockphoto.com

IN MEMORY OF

Michael Lamp, 1956–2013
and
Victor Buxbaum, 1961–2013

And though you want to last forever
You know you never will;
And the goodbye makes the journey harder still.
—*Yusuf (Cat Stevens)*

ACKNOWLEDGMENTS

The author wishes to thank the following publications, both in print and online, in which some of these poems first appeared, occasionally in slightly different versions:

Aberration Labyrinth: "Aging;" "Dust"
Aji Magazine: "In This Fallow Season;" "Requiem for a Fisherman"
Aleola: "The Awful Dominion of Brightness;" "Beginning the Story;" "Igneous Rock and the Church Picnic;" "Ingrid Jonker;" "The Reverend Igneous Rock Plays Chess with Death;" "The Widower Considers Candles"
Allegro: "Upon This Rock"
Ancient Paths Online: "The Forgotten Bees"
Apple Valley Review: "A Stand of Cottonwoods in a Field North of Colorado Springs;" "Part of the Equation;" "Train Whistle in the Dead of Night"
Big River Poetry Review: "Omens"
Bird's Thumb: "The Original Adam Forepaugh Shows"
The Bitchin' Kitsch: "Yeats and the Cockroach"
Blinders Literary Journal: "Erasure"
Breath and Shadow: "Absurdity for Drum and Glockenspiel;" "Reliquary"
Busting and Droning: "Aubade;" "Beneath the Southeast Light;" "Chinese Blessing Scam;" "Pulp Fiction;" "Worlds Beyond the Visible"
Clover: "Sunflower Sutra Haiku;" "Whale Skeleton"
The Concho River Review: "Distrusting the Stars"

The Cortland Review: "Rice Balls"

Dead Snakes: "The Reverend Igneous Rock Abandons National Poetry Month;" "Igneous Rock And Ignatz Mice"

Decanto: "The Only Angels;" "The Reverend Igneous Rock Presides at the Creation of the Universe;" "Torn;" "Troll"

Grasslimb: "Stillborn"

Leaves of Ink: "Soap Bubbles"

The Road Not Taken: "Dollhouse;" "The Wreck of the Edward (Sic) Fitzgerald"

The Same: "John Clare in the Madhouse"

Toasted Cheese: "Beginning a New Notebook"

Weird Cookies: "Mothball Fleet;" "Resonance;" "What Must the Dead Be Thinking?"

Work to a Calm: "At 56"

The Writing Disorder: "An Accident of Weather;" "After Thirty Years;" "Sable"

On a more personal note, I would like once again to thank Barry Sheinkopf for persuading me to compile this book, our second project together, and for his unflagging support and encouragement since the very early days of what has turned out to be a long and fruitful journey. As before, thanks and acknowledgment are also due to David Gwilym Anthony, Barbara Belle-Diamond, Bill Bly, Dan Brady, Barbara Brewer, Buford Buntin, Susan Burke, Diana Caliz, Marsha Campbell, Chris Charles, Peggy Clinton, Bobby Coleman, Robert Crabill, Eric Dahm, Owen Dunkle, Jack Foley, Hugh Gerstein, Louis Grace, Taylor Graham, Ryan Guth, Tom Hargarten, Johnny Hernandez, Jeff Kalmar, Sid Kemp, Ray Kerr, Eugenia Koukounas, Deena Larsen, David Lauter, Vincent Libasci, Kris Lindbeck, April Lindner, April Lindt, Marco Lule, Jeanne Lupton, Gary Mallin, Geraldine McGrath, Valerie Nance, Mr. Natural, Wendy Overin, Nathan Phelps, Kathy Reed, Janet Rhodes, Michael Rhodes, Robert-Harry Rovin, Daniel Ryan, Laurie Sato, Sally Love Saunders, Cindy Sawchuck, C. Lavett Smith, Marjorie M. Smith, John Strain, Linda Tabor-Beck, Jan Tilden, Sean Tripi, Ray Valdez, George Van Ausdall, Susan Van Ausdall, Vicki Van Ausdall, Christopher Watkins, Jennifer Whitten, Socrates Wilde, Janet Wildung, John Young, and Fritz Zimmerman.

AUTHOR'S NOTE

The majority of the poems in this collection are drawn from those I wrote between January 2013 and August 2014, although a few date from as much as six years earlier—scraps salvaged from an extended period of writer's block which, in retrospect, did yield one or two things I felt were worth saving. At the heart of things, there is an extended sequence that is earlier still.

Unlike my previous effort, *Smoke In Cold Weather*, these poems are not united by a single formal conceit—in that case, a gathering of sonnets—but instead, range much more widely, both in terms of style, and of subject matter. Hopefully, readers will discern a unifying voice here, although I confess I am not adept at recognizing the characteristics that set my writing apart from that of others.

It was never my intention to abandon the sonnet altogether. Rather, I aspire to move freely between traditional and free verse forms, without the transition being too jarring. Form, after all, should be employed in the service of content, and not vice versa. Reading my poems, I hope one will experience, first and foremost, an emotion, and that the literary devices, language, and imagery used to convey that emotion will seem natural enough to recede into invisibility, like the iambic cadence barely perceived beneath the lines of Shakespeare's sonnets, or the upright bass that lays the foundation for a Charlie Parker saxophone solo.

As in the past, I have deliberately eschewed any attempt to group these poems in a logical, or a chronological, sequence, preferring instead to construct a sort of verbal mosaic or collage, in which I have sought to place each poem so that it is as different from those adjacent to it as possible. I can't help feeling that the space between these surprising shifts in mood, time, and location—like the spark of a thought leaping from synapse to synapse—is one of the principal places where true poetry takes place. The book is divided into four sections, three of which are of roughly equal length, in an attempt to make it easier to access, but the mosaic approach holds true within each section, as it does overall.

I have included a series poems concerning a fictional character I invented more than fifteen years ago, the Reverend Igneous Rock. The poems are both humorous and satirical, and somewhat different in tone from the others. They also make up the largest of the subdivisions. I had originally envisioned publishing them as a separate volume but, after several years, have come to feel that I have traveled as far with the good Reverend as either of us is willing to go. Since some of these poems are beginning to appear in magazines, I see no reason not to include them.

The idea for Igneous Rock arrived in an Amtrak railway carriage stranded for what seemed like hours in the Utah desert, in response to a conversation I had with my late wife, Pat, while we were en route from San Francisco to Colorado to visit my parents. Pat, who was African American and had grown up in a traditional Black Baptist church, worked as an aide in science classes at a middle school. Admiring the view out the carriage window, she remarked on the various vividly colored striations in the rocks surrounding us, and asked how, if the Bible claimed that the world was only six thousand years old, these weathered columns and arches could date back millions of years. A spirited discussion about geological time ensued, and, in the course of it, I found myself using the term "igneous rock." No sooner had I said the words than I imagined a fire-and-brimstone preacher of that name. The section "Upon This Rock" had its genesis in this offhand bit of wordplay. Today, eight years after Pat's passing, it has become a kind of memorial to her.

The Widower Considers Candles looks both backward and forward. I have always experienced the poet's vocation as a journey, and I can't wait to see where it will take me next. I invite you to accompany me on this ongoing voyage of discovery.

Robert Lavett Smith
San Francisco
September 2014

Table of Contents

THE AWFUL DOMINION OF BRIGHTNESS

❄

DISTRUSTING THE STARS

❄

UPON THIS ROCK

❄

AN ACCIDENT OF WEATHER

❄

The Awful Dominion
of Brightness

❄

AUBADE

Every morning before summer school
as I sit alone in the classroom
waiting for the first bell, centering,
a student whose name I do not know
passes outside my window, singing loudly,
nonsense syllables spilling into the courtyard
still damp with dew—clear, untroubled notes,
as much a part of the breaking day as the smell
of rain on leaves, the heat
that licks the concrete as the fog disperses.

WILD BOAR ROLLING IN GASOLINE

In some parts of Spain,
my friend Carlos informs me,
hunters flush out wild boar
by filling dry riverbeds with gasoline,
then hiding in the underbrush
until the beasts come to roll
in a thick petroleum mud.

It cleanses them, he insists,
stripping dust and filth
from their coarse fur,
although I myself suspect
they may be more attracted
by the fuel's pungent stink.
"We wait until they've had their bath,"
he says, grinning,
"and then we shoot them."

BENEATH THE SOUTHEAST LIGHT

That weekend on Block Island, forty years ago,
lingers most vividly as an image I never saw:
on the pale sand beneath the bluffs near
the Southeast Light, our hosts told us,
legend had it that during the Pequot Wars
one tribe had driven another
over the precipice to their deaths,
the tide churning red on the rocks below.

Setting to work with shovel and pail,
my sister and I unearthed only the usual
cockles, knobbed whelk, and periwinkles—
and the occasional splinter of driftwood,
ancient and fissured, smooth in our hands.

But the locals insisted that sometimes,
even then, shards of human bone
would wash ashore, scoured
by salt and sea until they shone
like glass: grisly relics refashioned
by time into a sort of grim beauty.

SUNFLOWER SUTRA HAIKU

Rusted locomotive.
Ruined sunflower stands tall
against sunset hills.

—a nod to Allen Ginsberg, as rendered in the style of Basho

THE AWFUL DOMINION OF BRIGHTNESS

As when harsh light
flares on the chrome
of an abandoned car,
or ignites tenement
windows an instant
before sunset, pinpricks
burn through the film—
a glimpse of something
quivering beyond the scope
of any human language,
even prayer. Perhaps
this is what the prophets
really meant by God:
the awful dominion
of brightness.

A STAND OF COTTONWOODS IN A FIELD
NORTH OF COLORADO SPRINGS

Against a sky
flecked with cold light,
these gaunt trunks
and grasping branches
could be figures
in a book of hours,
emaciated saints
in the dying of the year,
resigned to some martyrdom
they alone foresee.
At their feet, scraps
of dirty snow are scattered
through the grass
like pages torn from a ledger
of judgments, their stern
sentences washed clean
by the weather, nothing
remaining in the early dusk
but a whiteness
as translucent as old vellum.

CHINESE BLESSING SCAM

A notice on the bus
warns the Chinese community
to beware of con artists
who persuade elderly women
they must pay for a blessing
to protect their homes,
making them, as it were,
the prey of prayers.
I consider Hui-Lan Cao,
the 86-year-old grandmother
of an autistic boy I tutor—
her veined, fluttering hands
the color of weak tea,
her frail frame contorted by osteoporosis—
hunched in the gloom of a converted garage,
a confusion of brown newspapers
and discarded medicine phials
so cluttered and filthy
as to be beyond the reach
of even a scammer's phony entreaties.

THE ONLY ANGELS

Every angel is terrifying.
—Rilke

The only angels I believe in,
the only true and reliable messengers,
are limestone figures softened by centuries
in salty Atlantic air,
the feathers of their folded wings
worn smooth at the edges,
their features indistinct
save for the yellow moss
that seals their eyes
like a quiet pentecostal fire.

FAMINE FOLLIES

We remember having glimpsed
these chimeras of brick and mortar
(oddly insubstantial for their solidity)
from trains or buses as we roamed
the furrowed English countryside,
never suspecting their dark histories:
how the term "famine follies,"
rolling so easily off the tongue,
recalled the Irish Diaspora,
destitution and blight.

They were in effect
the WPA projects of their day,
concrete wedding cake toppers
conceived as unapologetic nonsense
to provide labor for the dispossessed,
since the gentry distrusted outright charity.

Marble gazebos with fluted columns,
elaborately domed temples,
crenellated turrets bereft
of any encircling castle,
and perhaps most memorably,
highways leading nowhere—
truncated and *sans* destination—
ominously suggestive in their pointlessness,
their abrupt and definitive end.

DUST

i.m.: Patricia Lewis Smith, 1953–2005

You, gone nearly eight years now;
I, living alone in an apartment
comfortable enough save for the silence,
the loneliness that nightly settles
on everything like dust.

And like dust, that sense of loss
now and then wiped away, only to return—
although it is more than neglect
that dims your smile in every photo,
as over time accustomed caress and gesture
enter the realm of myth and speculation.

Slowly, the dust your body has become
reclaims the world you left behind;
even my own face, in a mirror,
seems a trick of light, indistinct as memory.

FROM THE PILGRIM'S JOURNAL

Chârtres Cathedral with its mismatched spires
rises from the unbroken plain of my thoughts
like a two-masted schooner adrift in a sea
of wheat and brown heat, calling to mind
an earlier summer and the first sight
of the pinnacle of Mont Saint Michel
dumbstruck among the quicksands,
the topaz sky precisely the color
of moth's wings the instant before
they're incinerated by the light.

AT A SCREENING OF A VIDEO MADE BY HIGH SCHOOL SPECIAL EDUCATION STUDENTS

Innocents always, they appear younger
than their adolescent years.

The crude paper masks
might have been made by kindergarteners,
and indeed they seem like children
adrift in bodies too big for them,
bodies already stubbornly blooming
into an unforeseen adulthood.

The film itself—fifteen minutes before a hand-held camera—
betrays their excitement, their nervousness,
more poignantly than do the cartoonish characters,
banal situations and flat dialogue
of this, their first screenplay.

But they're happy that you've come,
and somehow it's the missed or mangled lines
that ring the most true,
the hesitations and falterings
that make you want to clap the loudest.

STILLBORN

My father, thought an only child,
had an older brother, stillborn,
whose grave I was taken to see
once, years ago, when I was
certainly no more than seven.

I remember the tiny marble
headstone plainly engraved
with two words—Baby Smith—
and no dates, thrust through
pallid grass like a milk tooth.

And it occurs to me now,
all these decades later, that
as a child I was called Bobby,
a near echo, as though somehow
I carried a part of that old grief
with me into the world.

LIKE TIGHTROPE WALKERS

i.m.: Miles Woodbury Harrison, 1854–1924

It's said Miles and his older brother
walked the nine miles from Grafton to Oberlin
by following the railroad tracks, barefoot,
balanced on the smooth black rails
like tightrope walkers, fearless of the freights
that passed only rarely, even in the Seventies.

Their cousins were still tilling the land back then,
one horse or maybe two, chickens and a cow,
though no one now alive remembers
what crops they planted.

Presumably the house where
they stayed while at college
was torn down ninety years later
to make room for the new library.
Another story persists
of how embarrassed they were
coming down to breakfast that first morning,
since neither had thought to wear shoes.

The only physical evidence of their stay,
eventually donated to the archive,
is a rusty oil lamp on a hickory pole,
metal and wood worn the uniform brown
of late autumn, which one or the other
is rumored to have carried in vigils
protesting God only knows what
during the Reconstruction.

TROLL

At six I was a troll, so I believed,
living in an apartment
beneath the Whitestone Bridge,
College Point, Queens,
the year that Kennedy died.

Certainly I was short enough
to look the part, husky enough.
When I was tired my right eye turned,
shackled to its own orbit, an evil eye.
Prominent incisors complete the picture.

In school photographs from that period,
I always look distracted—
my good eye focused
on someplace in the distance
it seems that only I can see.

But mine has never
been a heart for mischief.
The child I was waylaid no strangers
beneath the great green bridge
that cleaved a fairytale sky.

MOONRISE, EARLY SEPTEMBER

If you want to write a song about the heart,
Think about the moon before you start.
—Paul Simon

On an ordinary evening meaning nothing
apart from whatever we bring to it,
for one particularly striking instant,
the lunar seas resembled a hand print—
as though the ripened moon were a stone
someone had grasped and thrown clear
of the horizon rotten with twilight,
into a sky where the first stars—
afterimages dead for millennia—
were stubbornly beginning to appear.

THE WRECK OF THE EDWARD (SIC) FITZGERALD

When I was still a teenager, I thought
The shipwreck nodded to the Rubáiyát;
I pictured quatrains strewn on frigid water,
And was dismayed to learn that it did not.

AT THE GRAVESIDE

i.m.: Genevieve Harrison Maple, 1900–1978

Beige dress, matching shoes:
Adrift in a sheen of silk
vivid as water, she didn't look
natural, a senescent Ophelia
swept away down the long,
dark river of her mortality.

But what I remember most
is lingering at the graveside
afterwards, in a light but steady
drizzle, relatives all departed
for the home of an elderly
aunt, Irish whiskey and a wake.

The undertaker, her high school
classmate, gaunt and gray as the rain,
raindrops bright as nails on the shoulders
of his black coat—I swear, I believe

to this day the man had entirely
lost sight of the fact that I was
a mourner—patiently explained,

with great pride, how the precisely
notched concrete cover of the crypt,
watertight beneath its own weight,
prevented moisture from penetrating.

SANCTUARY

The Cathedral of St. Gautiens, Tours,
its once-white limestone indelibly
dimmed by the soot of centuries
to a soiled khaki that seemed to echo
the sluggish depths of the adjacent
river Loire, was cool and shadowy
even on clear days, sunlight scattered
in bright fragments across the tiled floor
by the fanned glory of the rose window.
I was no pilgrim, certainly no penitent,
but sometimes I attended Mass there
back in the seventies, drawn by plainsong
and the ancient enigma of the Sacrament.
Groping through the gloom toward the rows
of folding chairs that served in lieu of pews,
I remember the stalwart columns flanking
the nave, their crowns lost in darkness,
splashes of lichen lurid and luminous
on their rough surface, how easily the soft
stone, powdering, came away on my hands.

JOSHUA'S ZEBRAS

Heat pools under the trees
at the far end of the enclosure,
beyond the cyclone fence.
In vain I scan the shadows
for the sleek striped shapes
I am certain must be there.

Joshua, fourteen and autistic,
cannot hide his disappointment;
we've walked the length of the zoo,
a quarter mile from the main gate,
with twenty middle-schoolers
because he wants to see a zebra.

And when the beasts decline
to make an appearance
the sadness in Joshua's eyes
is like the moist light
in the eyes of horses:
the quiet resignation,
mute acceptance of pain.

TORN

Vestis virum reddit.
　　　　　—Quintilian

There are holes in even my fanciest clothes
from frequent disputations with the earth.
Gracelessness has cultivated a long acquaintance
with stones, with grass.

And how can I hope to mend them
with hands as unsteady as these?
As well try threading starlight
through the eye of the risen moon.

Nights, warp and woof give way
like a dead language unraveling;
even so splendid a costume as memory
begins to fray—

style and cut decades out of date:
the fabric, dimmed by deepest solitude,
gnawed by insectile swarms of regret,
and every tear, a tear.

THE MARTYRDOM OF ALICE FROM DALLAS

Mary Alice Wade Julian, 1893-1955; sideshow performer

In a silver gelatin print from the twenties,
the flowered dress barely covers her massive thighs;
her legs, bulging like sausages stuffed to bursting,
are spread wide not out of immodesty or lewdness,
but to accommodate the vastness of her belly.

She perches uneasily on a threadbare armchair,
arms folded across her stomach in lieu of a lap;
her clasped hands resembling tiny white flowers,
surprisingly delicate given the width of her arms;
elbows invisible, buried in folds of pale flesh.

Occupying a three-sided wooden carnival stall
open only at the front, she could be a prize cow
offered for sale, or a hippo from the menagerie,
her humanity submerged in our awe at her girth.

As the camera has caught her, she's looking upward,
her broad features veiled in shadow, hidden eyes
fixed on something we ourselves can't see—
much as the martyrs in rococo murals turn their gaze
away from the sins of the world, to the hope of Heaven.

On the partition behind her, plywood letters
several inches high proclaim to all and sundry
the name by which she's most widely known:
ALICE FROM DALLAS (at over 685 pounds,
undoubtedly) THE WORLD'S FATTEST GIRL.

PART OF THE EQUATION

First, factor the diminished light
of early summer, when the days
begin to contract—shyly, as though
loath to acknowledge their dwindling.

Then, combine like terms:
The radiant aureole rimming a leaf,
more optimism than substance;
a hint of the colorless rigor of water.

Simplify the following expressions:
Shadows smudged slightly at the edges
like sidewalk pastels blurred by recent rain;
the sticky blue scent of hydrangeas in bloom.

Lastly, reduce the wrought-iron railings
scrawling their demotic terms
across the chalkboard green
of the library lawn,

where a solitary crow
pecks at something—
a feathered "X,"
an unsolvable variable.

TRAIN WHISTLE IN THE DEAD OF NIGHT

The tracks skirted the west side of town,
passing warehouses abandoned since the fifties,
clusters of single family homes with beveled porches
whose peeling façades were bandaged with tar paper,
crossing a green sea of cattails and marsh grass
that looked, in uncertain light, like an estuary.

This was a working class neighborhood,
worlds away from the gentrification already
beginning to assert itself along Washington Street,
the trendy bars, boutiques, and exotic eateries.
I had hardly ever been there, save once or twice
walking alone at dusk or just at dawn, as stars
either bloomed or faded in the rusted sky.

But in the dead of night, abruptly awakened beneath
the ornate tin ceiling of my room in the railroad flat
I shared, I often heard the long exhalation of a train,
mournful as a country song: some rattling old freight
lumbering through the dark to Bayonne or Newark,
laden with an unguessable cargo for the docks.

All this was thirty years ago, but lately,
waking again on the opposite coast
at that lightless hour when memory
is most persistent, I find I can distinguish,
as though in a dream, that moaning whistle,
tempting me back to a time I can never reclaim.

AMONG THE FOSSILS OF THE TONGUE

For a friend who cautions I live too much in the past.

Today I was asked by a student
whether I'd ever seen a panda.
Unbidden, an image leapt to mind:
the cuddly, saddle shoe body
rounded like a Saturday morning cartoon,
bright button eyes rimmed with darkness
but had I truly come face to face with one?
For the life of me, I couldn't say.

That's the past for you, remaking
itself without our leave, conjuring
scenes so vivid we're almost sure
they must have happened. And if I'm
a bit too preoccupied with entropy,
perhaps it's simply that I forage among
the fossils of the tongue, every word
slick with a tar of whispers and echoes.

AGING

The tiny insurrections in our bones,
resignation marshaling in the blood,
the mind like a city
sacked by invaders
an hour after curfew,
windows boarded up or broken,
a dozen small fires
blistering the horizon
as the rattle of crickets
fills the humid,
insouciant night.

SOAP BUBBLES

Loosed from a wire wand,
they drift indolently
over the playground
at the rehabilitation center,
glittering spheres of light
through which children
do an awkward but oddly
compelling dance. Some burst
on the rubber flagstones;
others vanish as quickly
as young hands try to grasp them;
the whole of the scene—crutches,
canes, and walkers, shrieks
of insouciant laughter—is mirrored
in the eyes of an autistic boy
who stands always to one side,
no expression on his features.
Bubbles tumble like stars
through an ocular darkness,
a deep and stagnant water.

SABLE

W. B. Yeats, the story goes,
young and impecunious in London,
rubbed lampblack into his stockings
to hide the rends in his boots.
Barely a century earlier, sailors
burned cauldrons of pitch on deck
to keep water-sprites at bay,
and I'm assured the India ink
generations have counted on
is nothing more than midnight's tallow
fat with the leavings of guttered fires.
In the middle ages, sable showed—
dare we say it?—its darker side:
blood pooling beneath fevered skin
lent a name to the scourge
that tested the piety of saints.
Notwithstanding, I trust the darkness:
moist flannel enfolding a summer night,
stars pinned like disappointments
to its unblemished mystery.

Distrusting The Stars

❄

WHALE SKELETON

The baleen brushes
between the great jaws
are so like the memory
of my grandfather's
shaving brush
that for a moment
it is possible to imagine
erect legions
of sand-scoured vertebrae
gleaming like porcelain
in the encroaching tide,
a lather of algae and kelp
softening the cheek
of the now-nearly-
submerged shoreline.

THE ORIGINAL ADAM FOREPAUGH SHOWS

Living statues on horseback,
Barlow and Amphett, two champion
horsemen, in daring illustrations
of celebrated statues, while riding
upon bare-back horses,

proclaims the crisp, vividly colored
reproduction of an antique
circus poster, doubtless rendered
several sizes smaller than the original—

a watercolor illustration depicting
performers painted the dusty pallor
of marble, plumed helmets, swords
raised as though in the heat of battle,

the whole of their costume white,
and (we imagine) perfectly still
atop their thundering pedestals
of tautly-muscled horseflesh.

How quaint the scene seems
in its carefully-staged intricacy,
the violence—the movement itself—
seen from sufficient distance now
to have become almost mythic,

as remote from our twenty-first century
as it must have been from the classical

poses it so seamlessly emulated.

And this in a world
no doubt already primed
for a war whose horrors
Edwardian gentility
could scarcely have imagined.

With what innocent optimism
the final line of text declares
(unnecessarily, as it seems to us),

Positively the 31st annual tour
of this great show.

ERASURE

The fog's so dense
windows brim
with a soggy whiteness
amounting to erasure.

I've never been persuaded
by the traditional image of Heaven:
concupiscent clouds and rosy light,
substantial radiance, splendor made flesh.

How much likelier it seems
that whatever lies beyond
resembles this roiling void,
brain-gray and bloodied

by a halfhearted dawn
that can't quite manage to break.
Sounds seem muted as well,
as after a deep snowfall—

like the indecipherable voices
my late wife must have heard
in the depths of coma, rumors
penetrating the heft of death—

or like the stutter of lightning
on a drenched horizon,
everything drizzle and shadow
as darkness starts to fall.

DISTRUSTING THE STARS

Look up at the stars and not down at your feet. Be curious.
—Stephen Hawking

Cerebral palsy having always
rendered my balance uncertain,
I learned early to pay attention
to things most people take for granted.
One misstep, a moment's distraction,
could send me sprawling.

I *do* look down at my feet,
purpled still by surgical scars
that emblazon the skin
with indecipherable hieroglyphics
written in pain on aging bone.

I look at my feet; I have to.
And on cold summer nights
by the Bay, fog worn away
and the sky crisp, I have also sometimes
considered the stars. But I distrust them,
how they withhold their beauty
at such an immeasurable distance.

PLACES LIGHT DOESN'T REACH

By early April, the sky
where setting stars still clung a week ago
has turned an opalescent glow
ripening above silhouetted poplars
through which neighborhood ravens dart,
feathered scraps torn from departing night.

For some reason the birds that populate this street—
blackbirds, crows, these raucous crepuscular angels—
all wear an impenetrable tincture of India ink,
the sheen of the nascent day
dripping from their wings.

We have been raised to praise the light,
but there is a beauty to places light doesn't reach,
an honesty that becomes apparent,
especially as one grows older.

The finality of darkness makes us thankful,
we who must one day unfailingly accept
even the bitterest of its gifts.

LIKE A BLACK HANDKERCHIEF

Above the backyard clothesline,
a bat, a black handkerchief snatched by wind,
flickered against a sky of deepening scarlet
while fireflies darted through unkempt grass
and trees bled gradually to silhouette.

It was a sticky summer night,
New Jersey suburb, late-1960s,
the final throes of an endless dusk.

This strange wild creature,
a momentary shudder in my recollection,
swept upward like charred paper from a bonfire,
hinted at unseen conflagrations,
its presence unsettling enough
that the stars, when they at last appeared,
seemed oddly remote, comfortless, and cold.

IN THIS FALLOW SEASON

Yesterday, impecunious in this fallow season,
I arranged for a gift—some DVDs you wanted—
to be sent on your birthday, topping that off
with a nice floral arrangement I saw no need
to clutter up with teddy bears or Mylar balloons.

Years, now, into this longing, I have come
so far from hopefulness there is no need
to speculate about your response to this bounty,
no point anymore in trying to pretend
such offerings will soften your obdurate heart.

No matter. What little I've learned of love
suggests we see it clearly only in memory,
suggests there comes a point in every life
when solitude is as certain as the scrimshaw
of winter branches on a bleached-bone sky.

What then? We give for the sake of giving,
for remembrance. And if every gift takes us
a little deeper into loneliness, it imparts as well
a bittersweet blessing, like deepening twilight
anticipating the splendor of the darkness.

AT MADAME TUSSAUD'S
ON FISHERMAN'S WHARF

At Madame Tussaud's on Fisherman's Wharf,
we stand not quite together in the gallery
of musical legends, the distance between us
more than the few square feet occupied
by life-like replicas of sequined stars—
the moment filled by the ongoing stalemate
of determined resistance and unabated longing.

You are more splendid than Madonna,
although I dare not say so;
more vibrant than Lady Gaga,
although tonight your head scarf
effectively conceals the fact
that you also have better hair.

Posed for a cell phone picture
taken by one of the docents
before the likeness of Elton John,
fingerprints of thousands of tourists
smudging the sheen of his grand piano,
I can feel the weather in the "friend zone"
dipping below absolute zero.

Bridging an unimaginable gap,
here, where in any case nothing is real,
the taciturn Sir Elton shines
in this windless, windowless room,
a beaming, pallid pillar of wax.

OLD BATTLEFIELDS

Anywhere in the world
they lie unmarked below our feet:
buried as much beneath
the heft of oblivion
as beneath root-pierced,
worm-writhing clay.

That summer in Normandy, for instance:
I strode bleached roads
that parted fields of barley,
guessing I was treading on the graves
of friend and foe,
bones bright as fish hooks
in the encumbering dark,
snagged in the heavy net of earth.

THE FORECAST

for my father

There is so much I will not get to say.
The end in sight now, though perhaps not near,
I bless the broken gift of each new day.
Like runoff from the Rockies, cold and clear,
Years, in a steady stream, drain from your brain.
Who guesses what you understand, or hear?
Occasionally, through persistent pain,
Shine glimpses of the man I used to know,
Who can't acknowledge what I can't explain.
This silence that engulfs us seems to grow,
Stripping the bones of language bare again.
Deep into May, the forecast calls for snow;
In insubstantial air, blue skies bleed gray.
There is so much I will not get to say.

CHAMBER MUSIC

Sarah, my niece, a talented violist,
Has come down from Fort Collins for a visit.
Together, we try to make the pieces fit;
She points out something that I nearly missed.
At seventeen, she's so much like her mother—
Her features, gestures, cadence of her speech—
That she evokes a past my Dad can't reach,
A tenderness they shared with one another.
Sometimes he calls her by my sister's name,
Corrects himself perhaps, on days he's lucid;
But he's grown old, and here she's still a kid;
He dimly senses things aren't quite the same.
Sarah plays through an unfamiliar piece;
Dad's lost among discordant memories.

RUM AND TONIC

Midsummer sunlight smolders in a glass,
Faint carbonation, with a wedge of lime;
Drinks and companionship at dinner time
To help the endless dusks more quickly pass.
Gathered around, his wife of sixty years;
His son who came a thousand miles to stay
Here, at the core of the diminished day;
And now a gentle granddaughter appears.
Misshapen fragments of their conversation
Shudder like tumbleweeds across the room:
Words he cannot untangle, they'll consume;
But he proves equal to the situation.
Deep in his throat, the spreading warmth of rum
Ignites things past—and darker things to come.

THEY DIDN'T FIND ANYTHING

At 86, the father I once knew
Before the weakness and the memory loss—
A relic of the intellect he was—
Is sometimes present for an hour or two.
My mother tells a neighbor on the phone
She's seen the scanner's neon-lurid image,
His brain's sufficient for a man his age,
He really *should* be healthy, tests have shown.
Listening in from an adjoining room,
I joke with Dad that when the scanned his brain
The doctors came up empty, one could say.
His old, familiar grin cuts through the gloom,
And for a moment, he's himself again.
"I'm not so sure I'd *put* it quite that way."

THE SPANISH CHANNEL

Dad tunes the T.V. to the Spanish channel,
Bewildered by a language he can't speak.
(The capsules in his hearing aids are weak;
It's doubtful he hears anything at all.)
Shrunken and faded in the big recliner,
He stares in frank confusion at the screen.
My mother, barely present on the scene,
Tries not to let his helplessness define her.
Exasperated now, he turns to me,
Quietly mouthing he can't catch the words.
When I explain, he grimaces ruefully;
I'm not sure what he has or hasn't heard.
This unintended pantomime would be
Almost amusing if it weren't absurd.

BEGINNING A NEW NOTEBOOK

This is the sort of thing, I imagine,
that someone like Billy Collins
could write an enormously popular
poem about—a non-event fraught
with symbolic potential. Let us
therefore consider the Moleskine,
legendary *cahier* of Hemingway,
Picasso, and Chatwin (proclaims
the accompanying historical
leaflet), all of whom undoubtedly
did something more significant
with it than whatever I am about
to do. I must not allow myself
to be in any way intimidated.
But there is still the prospect
of staring down that first blank page.

DEMONS

The venerable *Librairie Française*
in lower Manhattan served mostly
the Haitian community from across
the Brooklyn Bridge in the early eighties—
immigrant folk any of whom, if asked,
would fervently avow their Catholicism
but who, in the gloom of fourth floor
walk ups, in the dead of night, made
offerings, lit candles to strange gods.

By far the biggest sellers in our inventory
concerned the occult, thick paperbacks
from third-world countries whose pages
swarmed with dragons swaddled in flame,
brimstone demons flexing leathery wings;
among both customers and salesclerks,
belief in dark powers was commonplace.

Once, the morning after a disappointing
date, a co-worker who took evening classes
in software engineering offered to improve
my love life, provided I was willing to procure
the blood of a newly-butchered nanny goat.

But the incident impressed most indelibly
on my recollection of those years concerns
an elderly woman whose shriveled face
was the color of tea steeped with honey,
eyes keen beneath a confusion of white hair
thinned until little remained of it but memory.

She entered our doors one bleak November
evening, a regular customer, and making
her way to the spell books, began leafing
through a well-thumbed old *grimoire,*
then, slamming it shut abruptly, turned
and ran from the store, jostling shoppers
in her haste, screaming in tropical French,
"Too powerful! *Much* too powerful!"

INGRID JONKER

As if South Africa—blistered by the sun
of apartheid, chained to the lonesome
moan of the sea—*needed* an "answer
to Sylvia Plath," or its eyes sealed
by a swarm of black butterflies.

AFTER THIRTY YEARS

Helmer's, Washington Avenue, Hoboken

Carved wooden bar darkened by the weight
of a ponderous century, ornate scroll work
to which the grime of the late Victorian era
still clings: how little changed it all seems
since I lived nearby decades ago, although
the pert, twenty-something bartender says
everything was refurbished after a fire upstairs,
smoke and water having scarred the walls.

I savor again familiar smells of old varnish
and sunlight. The same elegant antique mirror,
silvered crystal brimming with shadows,
runs the length of the counter, behind the bar.
But whose is this stranger's face, skin wrinkled
and loosening, that peers incredulously back
through the glittering bottles of aged whiskey,
imported tequila, Fernet and Tanqueray?

FAR FROM DAYLIGHT

That summer, in a museum in Mainz—
Das Naturhistorische Museum, or some such—
we discovered in a back room, far from daylight,
mummified bodies, moldering linens unraveled
to reveal skeletal faces, skin impossibly shrunken:
fragile enough to be translucent, but stained by mold
or embalming the vivid azure of turquoise, eyeless lids
sewn shut like buttonholes on a newly tailored shirt.

MOTHBALL FLEET

Gray giants chained to slow brown water,
they thronged the river above the Indian
Point Reactor, a floating ghost town,
sad relic of another generation's war.

On Sunday drives, when I was a child,
I would observe them, a grim procession
stretching upstream toward High Tor: rank
upon steely rank arrayed in ragged light.

Fifty years later, the power plant smokestacks
still spew their plumes of superheated steam
into a thin sky, but the ships have vanished,
depleted by time and a nation's endless need.

Today, it is mostly the silence I remember,
the way no sound ever seemed to carry across
the beaten surface, hinting at a deeper stillness
I was much too young, then, to understand.

WHODUNIT

Friday nights
on public television,
Hercule Poirot
proves once again
that life is nasty,
British, and short.
But there is no one
to hold accountable
for this solitude,
no one to point
an accusing finger
at the twilight
drowning in a glass
of cheap red wine.
No chalk marks
trace the outlines
of my murdered heart.

WHAT MUST THE DEAD BE THINKING?

Diabetic for several years, I probably should
cut out the drinking, or at least scale it back;
at this age, the weight, grown stubborn, stays with me,
and my joints have begun to creak like petulant hinges.

What must the dead be thinking, if somehow,
from their dim kingdom, they are watching now,
commiserating on the body's inexorable slide
towards that chambered realm beneath the grass?

How familiar it all must seem to them—
the gradual incursion of a pale stranger
into the so-comfortable flesh, bleached
like a circus poster too long in the sun.

But oh, the wonders it advertised once,
painted in broad strokes of riotous color!
The fire eater, the knife thrower steadying his aim,
the sure-footed high wire walker who never, ever, lost
    his footing. . . .

DOLL HOUSE

i.m.: Patricia Lewis Smith, 1953–2005

The tiny rooms, immaculately furnished,
Stood for the home we never could afford:
The roll-top desk, the copper cookware burnished
And hanging neatly, each embroidered word
On the stamp-sized sampler hung above the couch,
The bed with its bright quilt. In miniature
Were gathered here the dreams she could not touch;
Her doll house dreams brought out the best in her.
These days, her ashes stain a windowsill
No larger than a matchbook: she is gone,
But in these things she loved there lingers still
Some essence rescued from oblivion.
Each elfin fixture resonates with loss,
And grief's the only tenant of this house.

REQUIEM FOR A FISHERMAN

i.m.: Bursal Cox, died circa 1969

I remember your smile
as you guided the rod
in my tiny hands,
pointing at a barracuda
I couldn't see
among the corals—
how I heard years later
your body had been
discarded, bullet in your brain,
floating face-down in the shallows
off Miami, mouth leaking
a billowing trail of blood
like a hooked marlin.

FOR THE FIFTIETH ANNIVERSARY OF "THE SOUND OF SILENCE"

On February 19, 1964, the song practically wrote itself.
—Art Garfunkel, from the liner notes

Hello, Darkness—you still there?
Paul's 72 now, with a bad comb-over,
Far more than fifty ways to leave a lover;
Now even Artie's lost his fabled hair.

As for the subway prophets, tags today
Are barely legible, inscribed by those
For whom rebellion's nothing but a pose,
Slackers who haven't got that much to say.

Give me instead the cadence of revolt
Scripted by poets, starkly effervescent,
Not by some semi-literate adolescent
Who'll catch a whiff of metaphor, and bolt.

MISSISSINEWA COUNTY

for Jared Carter

At the Municipal Library in Hoboken,
among moldering volumes of Wordsworth,
Byron, and Swinburne, their leather spines
cracked and flaking in the long neglect
of the reading room that smelled
of plaster dust and mold, I encountered,
in 1983, a single volume of contemporary
verse, published two years previously,
the crisp tan jacket lit by a solitary
sunbeam that tumbled through the high,
smoky windows. *Work*, the title admonished,
for the Night Is Coming. Drunkards
and gravediggers, walleyes and Klansmen—
John Keats could scarcely have been more
awed and humbled before Chapman's Homer
than I was before this vividly peopled rural
county, its dark heart coiled tight as a twister
howling through Masters and Faulkner,
the lightning of genius spitting blue at its edges.

Upon This Rock

❄

Upon this rock I will build my church.
—Matthew 16:18

UPON THIS ROCK

The Reverend Igneous Rock—
his broad features sweat-lit,
dark as volcanic glass—
thunders into the pulpit
like Black Moses,
his vast silk vest
rippling with certitude,
cufflinks flashing like indignant stars.
High in the choir loft
organ chords insistent as Armageddon
punctuate the rumbling syllables
of his prayer; the very roof beams
creak their loud *amens*.
Oh, let the sisters
in tight dresses
dance in the varnished aisle,
fluttering tambourines!
Let the old aunts
with their paper fans
swoon and chatter in tongues!
Let the tall silent ushers
throw wide the doors
that sunlight itself may bow
before a greater glory,
the rafters be thronged with hymns,
every note an angel spreading
trembling bright wings of sound!

THE CHARIOT OF IGNEOUS ROCK

It was already a classic
when Moses smote the waters.
Deep blue velour seats
spread to receive the Reverend's
ample form like a heathen sea,
a holy book thrown open.
The rounded hood, burnished and obese,
gleams smugly beneath the streetlights,
capped by a chromed ornament
aimed at eternity like a gun sight.
Tires whose scrubbed whitewalls
shine like spinning haloes
purr over the scarred asphalt,
past old men smoking on street corners,
hookers preening in tight leather skirts,
pool halls from whose dark interiors
pours a raucous, unholy music.
Surely some revelation is at hand.
The degraded world tonight
seems to tremble with satanic fire—
although in reality this may be nothing more
than the angry glow of the taillights
set like rows of unforgiving eyes
into the rolling leviathan's
enormous tail fins.

IGNEOUS ROCK AND THE BEAN PIES OF ISLAM

Their faces are shaded
by the brims of flat
straw boater hats,
their smiles bright quarter moons
risen in that darkness.
Crisp red jackets,
perfectly creased trousers
in candy cane pinstripes
make them seem more
like a barbershop quartet
lost in a bus station
than what they are—
emissaries of an alien prophet
whose blasphemies swirl
the hot sands of the soul.
Igneous Rock storms past them,
brushing aside the stacked
white boxes of baked delicacies,
pumpkin, sweet potato, bean.
Unsteady towers topple
to the sidewalk. The Muslim youth
aren't smiling now, but keep their cool.
The Reverend, a pillar of icy disapproval,
twirls his diamond-handled cane
before him; bewildering them as he passes
with the thundering declaration,
"Jawbone of an ass! "

THE REVEREND IGNEOUS ROCK PRESIDES
AT THE CREATION OF THE UNIVERSE

Six thousand years ago
(he's certain it wasn't
a moment more, or less)
and still somehow
he was there—
sure it was nothing other
than his appointed duty
to lend the Lord a hand,
or at least proffer some badly needed
advice, a little constructive
criticism. Whole worlds
spun fully formed
from his plump fingers,
spiraling into the infinite.
His stride spanned galaxies,
bursting nebulae reflected
in his perfectly shined shoes.
And through it all, God
stood by, smiling—as if
faintly amused. Though
even the Reverend Igneous Rock
quailed a bit before that overwhelming
splendor, that awful radiance.

IGNEOUS ROCK AND THE SINS OF THE FLESH

Beulah Rock is a strong woman,
bestriding her world
of teacups and *petit fours*,
pig's feet and collard greens,
like a colossus. With gold
pince-nez perpetually perched
on her prodigious nose,
she is a meet and proper helpmate
for the Reverend Igneous Rock.
Her face, lighter than his,
and wider, is forever overshadowed
by a broad straw hat festooned
with leaves, wax grapes
that sweat in the sanctuary heat
on long summer Sundays.
Beneath her staining cotton dress,
her massive bra and girdle
seem the bastions of chastity. But this is not
always so. Past midnight,
Igneous, his face lit with a glory
not entirely the Lord's, leads her to bed,
whispering hallelujah
as he draws shut
the beaded curtain—

!!!!!!!!!!!!!!!!!!!!!!!!!!!!!!!
!!!!!!!!!!!!!!!!!!!!!!!!!!!!!!!!
!!!!!!!!!!!!!!!!!!!!!!!!!!!!!!!!!
!!!!!!!!!!!!!!!!!!!!!!!!!!!!!!!!!!

!!!!!!!!!!!!!!!!!!!!!!!!!!!!!!!!!!!!
!!!!!!!!!!!!!!!!!!!!!!!!!!!!!!!!!!!!

ROCK AND BARACK

Elijah, the Reverend's thirteen year old son—
Fubu tee shirt, baggy jeans, baseball cap reversed
over tight cornrows, ear buds snug as snails—
dreams of meeting the new President.
His father confidently assures him
this must very soon come to pass,
since greatness (it's well known) seeks
its own level. In his mind's eye,
Igneous sees himself in the Oval Office,
hand in hand with the Commander In Chief,
mugging for the camera. Almighty God
glowers in Heaven—spitting thunderbolts,
jealous at being left out of the shot.

NAMING

The family name of course
was set in stone.
Christian names proved more difficult.
Lucius Rock, tenant farmer
in the Delta, 1940s,
was no student
of geology.
He christened his son
with a term he found
in a surveyor's report,
because he liked the sound.
And down the decades
the misnomers continued.
When Igneous became
a father himself, he insisted
on *Elijah*, an Old Testament name,
a prophet's name.
Beulah, who sang in the choir
and knew the Spiritual,
caught the musical reference,
but said nothing.
She put her foot down
two years later
when their daughter was born.
He suggested *Plymouth*,
after the first car
he owned in seminary.
They called the girl Myrtle Mae.

IGNEOUS ROCK IN PRAYER

Thank you, Lord,
for the twelve-year-old
single malt
stashed discreetly
behind the cellar stairs,
sipped in secret
when the wide red moon
is caught like a wafer
in night's dark throat.
Praised be the ways
this particular spirit
moves me.
Thank you, Jesus.
Thank you, Lord.

IGNEOUS ROCK AND THE LADIES' CHRISTIAN AID SOCIETY LUNCHEON

Sweet Jesus,
how many green bean
and mushroom soup casseroles
can one man consume?
Rows of bright Jell-O salads
jiggle wetly
in the florescent light
of the Parish Hall,
a host of Philistines
arrayed against him.
Plump glazed hams
crowd cardboard tables,
cloves studding their backs
like some dreadful martyrdom.
And all around him
a sea of flowered dresses
presses close; a dozen
disputations tangled
into a roar like a mighty tide,
a confusion of tongues
putting Babel to shame.

THE RADIO OF THE REVEREND IGNEOUS ROCK

It belonged to old Lucius
back in the thirties,
the arched wooden cabinet
staid and respectable
as a church door,
thick brown varnish
dimmed by decades of dust.
Igneous is grudgingly
fond of it, despite
the siren call of worldly pleasures
it potentially represents.
In the gnat-glow
of sultry summer twilights
he tunes it to the Gospel station,
a broadcast no doubt funneled
straight from Heaven.
The husk and crackle
of high winds in Natchez,
thunderstorms over Shreveport,
mingle with joyously blended voices
that seem to have descended
from a fairer climate,
a citadel of latticed light.

THE RESURRECTION OF IGNEOUS ROCK

On Easter morning
the sanctuary brims with lilies,
roses, daffodils nodding
like a profusion of damp
golden chalices. The organ
plays; the choir, robes
trimmed with blood-bright crimson,
sings with a single voice.
The Reverend Igneous Rock
stands tall in the pulpit,
linen suit crisp
with generous light,
tie clasp a silver cross
nestled in a shimmer of dark silk.
But his mind is elsewhere
as he gazes on his flock,
for he has had *the dream* again.
It is always the same.
The stone rolled aside,
he strides triumphant
into the biblical dawn,
the astonished women
rubbing their eyes,
their limbs still heavy
with sleepless grief.
Igneous moves in his own
radiance, wing tipped shoes creaking
beneath the hem of his garment.

THE BIBLE STUDY OF IGNEOUS ROCK

The exception *proves* the rule?
Lord, what were you *thinking*?

THE REVEREND IGNEOUS ROCK VISITS
THE SUNDAY SCHOOL

The presence of the senior pastor
cannot distract the children
from their new comic books,
in which Lord Jesus—
wearing his gentle forbearance
like a soft sheath of sleep—
bears the Rood in agony
through the jeering throng.
New ink stains the tips
of their eager fingers.
Little Thaddeus has of course
already penciled a goatee
over the Savior's ample,
middle eastern beard;
and on the whole the demeanor
of the class is something
less than reverent: behind
the Reverend's back, spitballs
and wadded candy wrappers
trace a wide arc across
the darkness of the blackboard.
Igneous assures his young parishioners
that Jesus loves them, secretly wondering
how this can be so. Above the dull roar
of grade school piety
Miss Jones pleads for quiet,
her eyes bright with tears.
But Igneous, in his magnanimous

heart, feels inclined to indulge
such youthful boisterousness—
at least at first. Surely there's
no need to go into what happens
as the lesson progresses, no reason
to linger over the incident
involving the rat, the thumbtacks,
the matches, and the glue. . . .

THE REVEREND IGNEOUS ROCK
PLAYS CHESS WITH DEATH

Cribbage is more his game,
although admittedly the intricately
carved chessmen—ancient ivory
yellowed to the color of charnel
house bones—are truly beautiful,
even if Igneous finds himself
disconcerted by the expressions
of abject horror on the faces
of the pawns, the Black
Queen's slaughtered eyes.

His shadowy opponent never speaks,
never hesitates. A chill fills the room
each time the Reaper raises a decayed sleeve
to make a move. The Reverend is down
both rooks, a bishop, four pawns,
and something else he can't identify,
too awful to mention.
The casualties are mounting steadily.

Igneous thinks this is another dream.

He *hopes* it is.

IGNEOUS ROCK AND THE FORTUNE TELLER

Heathen nonsense, surely.
But he's curious.
Besides, this poor soul
seems to need saving.

The creases of his upturned palm
are dark with shadowy portents.
And when the Gypsy smiles,
her gold tooth flashes
with its own arcane theology.

THE REVEREND AND MISSUS IGNEOUS ROCK LIE TOGETHER IN THE DARKNESS AFTER MAKING LOVE

Drained and exhausted, he idly twists
the Bakelite knob of the radio,
and music fills the soft purple twilight.
Improbably, it's a little Jewish man
from New York, harmonizing
with a sacred quartet.

This isn't the kind of thing
Igneous usually prefers,
and he's confident God doesn't either.
But he recognizes the Dixie Hummingbirds,
and Reverend Claude Jeter's flawless falsetto
floating above a buoyant bass.

So he lets it play—tenderly curling
one arm around Beulah's massive
shoulders as the scent of her body
mingles easily with the sweetness
of lilacs whose indolent blossoms
nod in the humid breeze outside.

IGNEOUS ROCK AND THE RUMMAGE SALE

Hat boxes whose yellowed labels
have faded to illegibility,
lampshades whose pleats
are furred with the dust
of decades of neglect,
cardboard cartons overflowing
with coat racks and cushions,
magazines years out of date—
the Reverend Igneous Rock
moves among the detritus
of our lives, like a saint
among the afflicted,
the low and leprous.
That which the years
have reduced to rubbish
will not be healed—
only passed along
through hands increasingly
forgetful, things we cherished
becoming the burden of strangers.
Peering from beneath the brim
of his richly ribboned felt fedora,
Igneous exudes a spectacular dignity—
but he has to *work* at it,
surrounded as he is by legions
of dented kettles, broken televisions,
and abandoned children's toys.

THE REVEREND IGNEOUS ROCK
WALKS ON THE WATER

It isn't the miracle
it at first appears.
In August, on the pavements
downtown, heat rises
in layers, pliant
as the waves that obediently
cradled Our Savior's unshod feet.
Metal curbs,
brown and smooth with age,
become the tentacles
of sea creatures
submerged beneath a surface
that writhes, in certain lights,
like an uneasy depths.
Here, Igneous moves
among the lost and destitute,
doing good works.
At times it seems
to those around him
as though his footsteps
leave behind a fading wake;
often he himself
feels as though nothing
holds him upright
but his faith.

CLIMBING JACOB'S LADDER

Rung by rung
the song gets sung,
notes like dark beetles
inching their way
up the ruled staves.

Uncomfortable in a folding chair,
the Reverend Igneous Rock
struggles to maintain the calm authority
of a biblical patriarch,
his pearled watch fob
shining with grim determination
in the stained light.

But in the higher registers
the brittle voices of elderly sopranos
erode the melody like years
of steady rain.

Despite the choirmaster's efforts,
the bedrock of the bass line
seems hewn from unsteady stone
in a country prone to earthquakes.

And in themselves,
the timorous gesticulations
of the maestro's hands
exhort no one to excellence.

On Saturday evenings,
only hours before the service,
this music always moves
Igneous Rock to prayer.

IGNEOUS ROCK AMONG THE INFIDELS

Igneous quietly laments his involvement
with the "Church Across The Way" program,
which has resulted in his reluctant attendance
at this strange and disturbing service.

Clearly these misguided souls
do not know the Lord.
Revealed Truth, by its very nature,
cannot be "liberal."

Every word of the sermon
makes him shudder.
The choir's scandalously underdressed
in blue jeans and tee shirts.

And there isn't a single cross
in the whole place.
It's probably no coincidence
their symbol features a flame.

IGNEOUS ROCK AND THE CHURCH PICNIC

The subtle dance of sunlight and shadow
in the leaves overhead makes Igneous smile.
Heaven, perhaps, is something like this.

Down by the water, the voices of his flock,
softly singing treasured hymns,
mingle with the quiet stirrings
of a warm summer evening.

For a moment he can almost forget
the fly ball hit into the wasp's nest,
Sister Agnes's potato salad
through which an entire colony of red ants
scurried like demented paprika,
even the nature hike
that resulted in half the congregation
contracting a rash and an unholy itch.

As night falls,
he thinks with surprising tenderness
of the bloody noses and bruised knees
that bloomed among the youngsters like stigmata.

Shall we gather at the river?

We'd better.

And bring the calamine lotion.

IGNEOUS ROCK AND THE PANHANDLER

What a contrast between these two!
The Reverend in perfectly pressed gray flannel,
ascot pink as a summer dawn,
spats the pure white of redemption itself
crowning his immaculate shoes.
The stranger unkempt and unshaven,
smelling of gin mills and soup kitchens—
smelling of worse things, even, than that.

Igneous knows what the fellow needs.
They speak together in tones too low
to be overheard. Something we can't see
is angrily declined. Disappointment,
agitation are clearly visible
in the set of the man's shoulders.

As the vagrant turns to go,
Igneous offers his hand in vain;
opals and garnets glitter on his fingers.
A discarded leaflet announcing
an upcoming prayer meeting
flutters a moment in the gutter,
like a broken bird.

IGNEOUS ROCK PERFORMS A BAPTISM

A tiny brown face,
wrinkled and squalling,
peers over swaddling clothes,
seeming impossibly old.

Eyes screwed tight,
the infant flinches
as blessed Salvation
descends in a sprinkle
of frigid water.

Igneous is in fine voice this morning.
In his most sonorous tones
he poses the question,
"What have you chosen
to call this child?"

Cornelius Cuthbert Wilberforce Walker?

Igneous smiles benignly
as little Cornelius,
perhaps overwhelmed by the Holy Spirit,
lets forth a high, piercing wail.

Called forth into the Kingdom,
the kid permeates the chancel
with the pungent stench of the earth
whence his little body came.

IGNEOUS ROCK CONFRONTS HIS DOUBTS

They are not entirely
theological in nature.
Nor is he quick
to cotton to them.

The fundamentals, of course,
are beyond dispute:
the virgin birth, ministry
and miracles, apparition
wounded but living
on the road to Emmaus.

Yet niggling little details,
everyday difficulties,
are troublesome.

It isn't so much the big questions:

Why is there suffering
in the world? Is fat necessary?
Why are innocent babes
sometimes taken so early
into the hungry mansions
under the grass?

(These are imponderables
doubtless propounded specifically
to challenge his faith.)

But consider:

Why does the phone always ring
as soon as he's in the shower,
the doorbell chime insistently
the instant he's poured milk
over a bowl of crisp cereal?
How come the Lord made hemorrhoids,
ingrown toenails? And *where*
has Satan hidden his car keys?

Tenets he cannot reconcile
trouble his sleep.

Like doubting Thomas,
Igneous places trembling fingers
into the gash in his Savior's side.

THE FUNERAL

A dozen black hats,
modestly ribboned,
nod at the graveside, dim blossoms
stirred by a hesitant wind.
Hymnals bound in dark calf
flutter in gloved hands
like a murder of crows.

Outdoor burials are
always the most trying,
especially in a light drizzle,
under a sky so dark
the heavens themselves
seem attired in mourning.

The Reverend Igneous Rock
pauses in his remarks
long enough to wipe his glasses,
musing to himself
that nowhere in the Bible
is the sky described as blue.
All the same this sullen weather
bodes poorly for an entrance
into Glory.

His text is opened
to the twenty-third psalm,
the bright cream pages
pearled with raindrops.

He begins again:

The Lord is my Shepherd. . .

Just then, a peal of distant thunder
sounds, almost as if in reply.

. . .I shall not want. . .

So much, O Lord, is wanting
in this poor world.

IGNEOUS ROCK
AND THE DRUNKENNESS OF NOAH

And Ham, the father of Canaan,
saw the nakedness of his father,
and told his two brethren without.
—Genesis 9:22

A favorite Bible story,
especially when reading
to the children. How clearly
it demonstrates that even
the holiest have their foibles,
that sin can sneak up on
the most righteous of men.
But Igneous is always puzzled
by Ham's implied admiration
for his father's nakedness,
the exaggerated dismay
of Shem and Japheth, and
most of all by the snickering
this part of the tale almost
unfailingly engenders among
his pupils, particularly the older
boys in the back of the room.
He's prayed about this, fearing
perhaps he's overlooked some subtlety
in the narrative. But so far the Lord
has remained strangely silent
concerning his repeated entreaties.

IGNEOUS ROCK CONTEMPLATES
HIS CONGREGATION

Nearly nine hundred strong.

Two services on Sundays.

Three on major holidays.

The neighborhood is urban,
staunchly working class,
predominantly African American,
somewhat down at the heels.

Worshipers who bustle and jostle
through the heavy wooden doors
each Sabbath are many colors:
youngsters whose bright faces
shine with youth's fresh light,
couples still blushingly in love,
feeble pensioners who shrink
into shadow the way some flowers
tighten and withdraw
at the end of a weary day.

The Reverend Igneous Rock
welcomes them all.

IGNEOUS ROCK STRONGLY SUSPECTS
STEAM HEAT WAS INVENTED BY THE DEVIL

Vivid saints and angels,
heads bowed beneath leaded haloes,
smile benignly down
upon rows of overburdened pews
where young and old adjust cushions,
fidget, unfold paper fans
that shine in the humidity
like newly risen moons.

Beneath ornate bronze vents
that punctuate the shiny hardwood aisle,
steam groans and rumbles
like some rough beast
stirring at the heart of the world.
Sometimes, to his annoyance,
its moist baritone competes
with the Reverend Igneous Rock's
piously rumbling bass.

The incandescent blossom
of the rose window
blooms overhead in a firmament
as wide and commanding
as Heaven itself.

But on cold winter mornings
its bright glass sweats
in a most undignified manner,

trembling and indistinct
through ribbons of rising warmth.

THE REVEREND IGNEOUS ROCK RIDES THE SUNDAY SCHOOL BUS

. . .there appeared a chariot of fire. . .
—2 Kings 2:11

Many churches in the South
have buses painted hopeful colors,
emblazoned with Old Testament names
like Ebenezer and Ezekiel.

They're usually relics of a sort:
at least a generation out of date,
corners rounded like the shoulders
of antediluvian refrigerators.

The roofs of these venerable vehicles
are always unpainted, perhaps
to ward off the pitiless stare
of a Jehovah sun.

Diesel angels ferry cargoes
of souls through the years, spewing fumes,
trailing dirty streaks of oil
behind them on the road to Armageddon.

As they approach down the bleached tar
of some forsaken back road,
they shimmer and flare in hard light;
haloed, ablaze with righteousness.

And settled into the wide rear seat

of one of them, as though ensconced
upon the left hand of God, Igneous Rock
surveys his charges with a Cheshire cat smile.

The good Reverend struggles to maintain
an air of beneficent dignity, despite
the ill-fitting Bible Camp tee shirt
tight as cellophane across his heaving chest.

His rich bass dissects the laughing
songs of children, stumbling a little
over sometimes puerile lyrics
scarcely appropriate to the liturgy.

And not a single one of the ninety-nine
bottles will descend from that melodic
wall, silenced as they quickly are
by the frown clouding his countenance.

THE REVEREND IGNEOUS ROCK
DREAMS OF THE GATES OF PARADISE

The line is longer than he expected.

Much longer.

Of course, Igneous can't help
but find this encouraging,
from a pastoral point of view.

But he has to worry whether
there will be adequate parking
along the golden cobbles
beyond these pearly gates.

Saint Peter, a gray and tired angel
with the air of a harried clerk,
seems tried to the limits of saintly patience
by some disturbance up ahead.

Two elderly women, bearing
smug self-importance before them
like a battering ram, have forced
their way to the front of the line,
loudly proclaiming their own virtues,
eying other supernal suppliants
with undisguised disdain.

The elder, light-skinned and frail,
with haggard features that can never
have been as beautiful as she thinks,

is clearly in charge. She elbows
her way past Igneous before
the astonished Reverend can manage
to sputter a word of protest.

Her sister, darker and beefier,
at least mumbles a halfhearted apology
as she treads heavily
on the Reverend's unshod foot.

Igneous winces, his celestial body
surprisingly attuned to physical pain,
but decides to let the matter drop.
(This is hardly the moment, after all,
to risk making the wrong impression.)

Saint Peter, looking suddenly older
Than his two millennia,
Runs a weary finger
Down a page of his enormous ledger
And shakes his head.

The women protest shrilly.
There must be some mistake.
Their sorority sisters, they insist,
are already inside, expecting them.
The very sky would shake with lamentations
should they be turned away.

As Igneous looks on, bemused,
Saint Peter sighs,
and lets them enter.
There are worse sins, surely,
than their petty vanity.

IGNEOUS ROCK AND HIERONYMUS BOSCH

Painting, so the good Reverend
has always been told,
nourishes the soul.

Still, this *Garden of Earthly Delights*
isn't quite what he expected.

Granted, it's no more raucous
than certain street corners
in his neighborhood
at 3:00 a.m. on Sundays
after the bars close.

But here he sees sparrows
larger than elephants
casting hideous shadows
over a couple about to embrace,
the pair lewdly sprawled
across sunlit grass
that throbs like a sea of green fire.

On and on it goes:
a giant oyster from which human legs
protrude, twitching in agony.
A man riding an enormous sow
around the rim of a sullen lake.
People trapped in greasy bubbles
or within the rinds of bloated fruit.

Lord only knows what those buildings are
that pierce the sky like towering bottles
of some wanton foreign perfume.

Perhaps this abomination is meant
to warn of the perils of luxury.
Or maybe it's just a cruel joke.

Igneous shudders. He doesn't know art,
and at this rate, might well prefer
to keep it that way.

THE REVEREND IGNEOUS ROCK
RIDES A TRAIN THROUGH THE BADLANDS

The carriages are paused
on a railroad siding
outside Helper, Utah,
as the sun comes up.

By the side of the track
weathered telephone poles
lean into years of wind
like some vast crucifixion
stretching to the vanishing point.

Beulah and the kids,
scrunched into seats much too small
by means of incredible contortions,
snore peacefully around him—
a sound like dry air
rattling coarse desert scrub.

Somewhere beyond the line of sight
an eighteen-wheeler groans
along a distant highway.

Other than that,
the silence in the world
is the unfathomable silence
of the mind of God.

Mesas and arches of weathered rock—

banded red, green, yellow, and brown—
shine in the new light.

Day breaks, and the Reverend Igneous Rock,
a satisfied smile curling his lips,
slides into a doze, congratulating himself
on having been born
into so satisfactory a life.

i.m.: P. L. S., 1953–2005

THE REVEREND IGNEOUS ROCK CONTEMPLATES THE PREVALENCE OF DESPAIR

A sense of melancholy
is something Igneous understands
only in the abstract—
it has never really troubled him.

He is, after all,
respected by his community,
his family and friends.
Surely there can be no doubt
he is respected—admired—
even by God.

But in his pastoral work
he has often seen sorrow
in the faces of others:
the broken, the bereaved,
gaunt shades who pass
in the littered street,
listless, seemingly untouched
by warm Spring sunlight.

Ah, well. Igneous assumes
there is a reason for it all.

But sometimes—just sometimes—
he's not so sure.

IGNEOUS ROCK AT THE FOOT OF THE CROSS

The Sunday School Bibles
with soft leatherette covers—
black for boys, white for girls—
have an appendix at the back
containing maps of the Holy Land,
glossy full-color reproductions
of various Biblical scenes
as painted by the old masters.

The Reverend Igneous Rock
has one on the bookshelf
above his desk, to which he turns
for inspiration on long afternoons
of sunlight and stillness.

Thumbing idly through bright plates
by Rubens, Delacroix, and Titian,
he finds his eye abruptly drawn
to a figure greatly resembling himself
in the throng of anguished mourners
at the base of the freshly planted Rood.

He isn't particularly surprised.

In truth, it may be
that the broad Moorish face,
eyes turned upward in supplication
toward the Savior's bloodied brow,
is only a Jew whose features

have been darkened by centuries
of censer smoke and grime.

But it seems somehow right
that he should have been there,
his trembling hand extended
as though about to touch
the wounded feet through which the spike
blooms in its garnish of gore.

And there can be no doubt
that the Lord, pinned in His agony,
bestows upon this particular servant
a look of special approbation,
fondness, unconcealed pride.

IGNEOUS ROCK AND THE INTERFAITH TUESDAY NIGHT BOWLING LEAGUE

For so solid a man
the Reverend Igneous Rock
moves with surprising agility,
his stance and form as perfect
as though immortalized
in some flawless masterpiece
of pagan statuary.

His reflection, caught
in the waxed glow
of the lane beneath his feet,
lends his delivery the aura
of a minor miracle,
as though he were walking—
no, *dancing*—on water.

Glittering like a night sky
lit by a thousand stars,
his bowling ball thunders
toward the waiting pins.

Three remain upright,
reminding him for a moment
of crosses on Calvary.

Of course this image
has theological implications
it might be unwise to consider

until he's more suitably attired.

There are things a man
in a puce shirt with the name "Iggy"
embroidered in script above the pocket
feels unprepared to contemplate.

Be that as it may,
the wooden martyrs
wobble, but stand firm.

As the automated rack
descends to retrieve them,
they resemble robed white figures
lifted into darkness
like souls mounting to Heaven.

THE REVEREND IGNEOUS ROCK BEARS UP

The good Reverend Igneous Rock
Was never one given to shock
But is, I'm afraid,
Much more than dismayed
By some of the sins of his flock.

There are those whose love of the Lord
Gets twisted to something untoward;
Folks who—for their piety—
Still covet variety,
Have urges that can't be ignored.

Their Pastor, their mentor, and friend
Sometimes has his hair set on end
By stories he's told
That freeze his blood cold,
Confessions no penance can mend.

He sighs, and gets on with his life;
Goes home to his children and wife;
Suspects that some prayers
Catch God unawares,
Sparks struck on the edge of a knife.

THE REVEREND IGNEOUS ROCK ABANDONS
NATIONAL POETRY MONTH

> *"As to the amount of strain on the intellect now.
> Was you thinking at all of poetry?" Mr. Wegg inquired, musing.
> "Would it come dearer?" Mr. Boffin asked.
> "It would come dearer," Mr. Wegg returned.
> "For when a person comes to grind off poetry night after
> night, it is but right he should expect to be paid for its weakening
> effect on his mind."*
> —Charles Dickens, Our Mutual Friend

The Psalms have always
been good enough for him.

This new stuff doesn't make sense.

Why, for instance, is April,
season of lilacs and gauze-pale skies,
the "cruelest month," unless
it has something to do with income tax?

And how much could *possibly* depend
upon so insignificant a thing
as a red wheel
    barrow
probably already forgotten
by the unseen farmer—
and maybe even by the poet,
since it only seemed to warrant
eight short, simple lines?

Fog, as far as he knows,

doesn't *have* feet,
feline or otherwise.

And some poems he finds
even more ominous
and disturbing.

Take Allen Ginsberg, whoever he is.
Igneous knows the King James Version
chapter and verse, fore and reverse,
from beginning to end,
but can't help feeling
that something besides the righteous
indignation of the Old Testament
may underlie the bit about a

> *partition in a Turkish bath*
> *where the blond and naked*
> *angel came to pierce them*
> *with a sword...*

(The precise theology
and scriptural sources
inspiring this particular passage
continue to elude him.)

Frost, he remembers at the inauguration,
Reading his wind-blown verse before the nation.
(No one could make much sense of it, it's true—
But at least it rhymed, and had a rhythm too.)

The Belle—of Amherst—
Makes him think—
Of members—of his flock—

Secretly much—consumed—by Drink—
But never—prone—to talk.

Still, he draws the line at—

> *What a thrill——————*
> *My thumb instead of an onion.*

The rest—*red plush, hinge of skin*—
is quite disgusting, and written
by a woman, no less!

The good Reverend pushes
the library books aside
in despair, bewilderment, and revulsion.
Perhaps the Sunday School
will have to do without a special reading
by their Senior Pastor in honor
of National Poetry Month.

Alone in his darkening study,
Igneous takes down
his well-thumbed Bible
and begins to recite aloud.
His voice, rich as warm molasses,
fills all the shadowy corners
of the room:

> *Yea, though I walk*
> *through the valley*
> *of the shadow of death,*
> *I will fear no evil. . .*

THE REVEREND IGNEOUS ROCK, PREPARING THE HOMILY, FACES A SERIOUS WRITER'S BLOCK

Friends, I am reminded this morning
of the suffering of Uriah—
    —Joseph—Jehoshaphat—
    —Hezekiah—(?)—*Bud?!!!*

~~Friends, looking out at your familiar~~
~~faces this morning, I am (gratified?)~~
~~(alarmed?) (stricken?) (hungry?)~~
~~(slightly flatulent?)~~

Brothers and sisters, we are faced
    today with a crisis of
    immense proportions, which is—
        —*is?—is?!!!!*—

No one among us can have failed
    to notice—to be aware—

My dear brothers and sisters in Christ,
    the Lord once said to me—

(Maybe open with a joke?)

      Two apostles walk into a bar—

      Peter, I can see
      your house from here—

—but you didn't have holes—

(No. Do NOT open with joke!)

These are dark days
for our poor world.

On this glorious morning
I am reminded
how grateful I am
simply to be among you.

THE REVEREND IGNEOUS ROCK DISCREETLY ADMIRES THE MOST AMPLE OF WOMEN

Bear witness, O body in bloom,
to the goodness of the Lord
and to the wealthiness with which
He endowed thee.
        —Alan Ansen, *"Fatness"*

It's no sin, he supposes,
to appreciate the *range* of pulchritude
so long as one doesn't
actively covet it.

But why are so many men so drawn
to these pale, emaciated girls
mincing through life on spindly legs,
whose tiny breasts swell timidly
beneath thin blouses, no more assertive
than pustules from mosquito bites?

Let us instead commend corpulence.

Beulah Rock is a large woman
whose unrepentant belly and pendulous teats
part the teeming throng around her
like Moses throwing wide the gates
of the reluctant sea.

Indeed, the rippling of her thighs
as she rocks forward into the world
recalls the restless surge of salt water,
a concupiscent tidal wave of flesh.

Each morning the bathroom scale
groans beneath the burden of her beauty,
needle thrust flat against the unknown country
beyond the far end of the dial.

Beulah waddles when she walks,
the cheeks of her great ass
rolling beneath her flowered skirt
like twin moons orbiting each other.
Igneous admires this, although he's careful
not to actually tell her so.

Her endless diets,
never openly discouraged,
privately make him shudder—
although he takes solace in the certainty
that each will leave her heavier than before.

A fetish? Perhaps.
Igneous doesn't trouble himself
about that. What is a man of God
to do but fall on his knees,
stuttering praises for this carnal bounty
so freely given of the Lord?

BREAD

On rainy Sunday afternoons
after the second service
Beulah and Myrtle Mae
bake bread in the shadowy kitchen,
the moist air warm and thick
with the beneficent smell
of rising dough.

Moon-pale loaves
deepen to chestnut,
their broad backs split
by the alchemy of ovens.

Against a worn slate sky
rain scrawls obscure hieroglyphics
on the windows; wind hurriedly
erases them again and again.

Myrtle, at ten already
broad and unyielding
as her mother, kneads
a soft white mass
dusted with flour
in dark, plump hands—
a limp doll gone heavy
with sullen dreams.

Beulah, her bright palms ghosted with yeast,
watches her daughter distractedly;

neither of them speaks.

Perhaps the silence of Heaven
is like this: the old house
settling like some indolent beast
around them, a slow creak
somewhere in its bones.

STAINED GLASS

Metal fatigue and a century
of gravity's relentless tug
have loosened the lead
tracing the glowing wings
of the cherubim who throng
the historic rose window;
the bright hosts attendant
at Creation have begun to sag;
the heavenly firmament itself
is buckled and slightly askew.
The Reverend Igneous Rock,
never one to pass up a chance
to see symbols and portents
in the most mundane details,
finds himself wondering sometimes
whether Heaven above hasn't begun to cave
under the pressure of so much virtue,
so much unredeemable vice—
whether that glorious Kingdom
beyond the disappointed tent of sky
hasn't begun to crack at the seams.
No matter. Things are what they are,
even in the Realms of the Spirit.
The crookedest, most battered halo
still blesses the world with its tarnished light.

IGNEOUS ROCK WEIGHS HIS OPTIONS

As a child he sometimes wanted,
as children do, to change his name,
hating the ponderous polysyllabic lump
that called forth teasing in schoolrooms.

He longed then to trim his moniker
at least a little, thinking perhaps
of *Ignius*—as much to say but less to write—
a centurion's name, magnificently Roman.

And of course there was Saint Roch,
that holy appellation a cornucopia
of variants: *Rochus, Roc, Rocco, Rok, Roko*.
The boy's head swam with possibilities.

His evangelical parents dismissed all this
as Popish nonsense. When he offered to cleanse
their sharecropper's shack of *la peste*
(a term he'd found in a schoolbook,

and which he hoped sounded ominous),
they called him a "pest" himself, and sent him
to the porch, where he shucked black-eyed peas
until his little hands were numb.

IGNEOUS ROCK AND IGNATZ MICE

> *It's wot's behind me that I am.*
> —Krazy Kat

He remembers the comic strip fondly
from a strange little book he found
while playing in his grandmother's attic
as a boy: the faded cardboard covers
warped, the curiously wide pages intact
although disfigured by a brown
blossoming of water stains.

From the first words,
this unassuming volume
spoke to him—directly,
without artifice or pretense:

> *Krazy Kat was a simple soul*
> *who didn't understand much*
> *that went on around him.*

A few years later, on Saturdays
at the local matinée,
he laughed with schoolmates
as the antics of Mrs. Quakk Wakk and Offissa Pupp
flickered across a buckled screen.

But it was Ignatz Mouse
whom Igneous most loved—
perhaps because the broken name

so closely mirrored his own;
perhaps because Krazy Kat,
her very gender shifting and ambiguous,
her dialect all jumbled vowels,
was apt to refer to her crony
as "Ignatz *Mice*,"
somehow suggesting multitudes
contained within one tiny form.

Mostly, it was the name.
As a young child, Igneous
had disliked his, reshaping it
through endless permutations
into things his restless childhood
might find an easier fit.

But like Ignatz, he had come to see it as:

> *A name with euphony.*
> *A name with harmony.*
> *A name with dignity.*

It was not until many years later
That Igneous, well into middle age
and pastor of a thriving church,
discovered that the cartoonist,
who signed his drawings simply "Herriman,"
with a scrawled "H" whose multiple crossbars
resembled the rungs of a ladder,
had been a man of color, a Creole
from New Orleans whose parents,
of French descent, had been listed
in the registries as mulattos.

Again, the suggestion of multitudes.
Igneous felt an even closer kinship
with Ignatz Mouse because of that.

But, although the Reverend Igneous Rock,
in the boundless charity of his Christian heart,
would be loath to admit it,
there is also the matter of the bricks.

To return to that book
he loved in childhood:

> . . .when Ignatz was annoyed
> he threw bricks. In fact,
> Ignatz threw bricks when
> he wasn't annoyed. He just
> couldn't help it.

Igneous Rock always chuckles
when he recalls that pearl of wisdom.

The Reverend is not
a mean spirited man.
Not in the least.

But he likes it.

He just *does*.

THE REVEREND IGNEOUS ROCK DISLIKES
RECEIVING A CD BY YUSUF ISLAM

It was given to him
by one of his parishioners,
an "old hippie" type.

Music is music, after all,
and in its way
it *does* praise God.

Still. Yusuf Islam.
Joe Muslim. Who does
this guy think he's kidding?

But Igneous smiles to think
there was another guitarist, a Charlie
Christian, back in the thirties.

IGNEOUS ROCK IN THE LAND OF DEMONS

"There are a lot of demons
out there today, brother!,"
calls the stranger whose yellow eyes
protrude from his gaunt, stubbled face.

He meets the Reverend's gaze
as Igneous passes,
opaque pupils
two clouded moons
that have never set
on the country of sleep.

Sharp June sunlight
stabs the scarred pavement—
the *scared* pavement,
one might almost say,
so worn and wounded
is the ancient asphalt.

And indeed, there are demons
everywhere this afternoon.
But Igneous Rock knows by now
not to expect horns
hidden under innocent fedoras,
tails curling discreetly
down a pants leg or beneath a skirt.

They are the twitching of lips
cracked with long thirst,

the despair in sagging shoulders
that might have known wings.

They are everywhere,
and the blind man
sees them more clearly than anyone.

Igneous pauses and turns back,
pressing a five dollar bill
into a hand that instantly closes
like a night-blooming flower.

IGNEOUS ROCK BUYS A CARVED MASK FROM GHANA AT THE LOCAL FLEA MARKET

An impulsive purchase,
not motivated by any
sudden desire to connect
with ancestry or roots.

Basically, the Reverend,
for reasons he doesn't entirely
understand, just took a fancy
to this curious thing.

Perhaps it's the colors.
It must be. Unlike other
African carvings he's seen,
this one is brightly painted.

Vibrant yellows, blues, and reds
enliven the dark wood: stretched cheeks
pale as ripe bananas, a blue diamond
ornamenting a high, pointed forehead.

It is pagan art, but Beulah
will like it, he surmises,
unless perchance it turns out
to be a fertility fetish.

As Igneous pays and wends his way
through the milling crowd,
a jocular parishioner calls to him,

"Why the long face?"

Even this flaccid pleasantry
can't spoil his sudden jubilation.
There are objects we seem meant to own
for a time, never knowing why.

In a sense, they are not really ours.
But their presence in our lives
blesses us, and they linger awhile
before inexorably moving on.

IGNEOUS ROCK AND THE COLLECTION PLATE

Plate, indeed.
A scratched veneer of darkening silver
over some common metal, probably brass.
And the worn circle of purple velvet
that serves as lining, thinned by poverty
and long usage to a cloudscape
where a few dull coins
shine like listless stars.

But for the Reverend Igneous Rock
this battered collection plate epitomizes
the humble beauty of God's Kingdom,
dented as it still is—after fifty years—
from the afternoon it winged the altar
when he and some kids from the Bible School
used it as a Frisbee in the empty sanctuary,
Eddie Morgan managing a spectacular catch,
the whole gang incurring the wrath
of dour old Pastor Horner
until the day he went to his reward.

THE REVEREND IGNEOUS ROCK
ANTICIPATES THE JUDGMENT DAY

He has imagined
the whole scene
so many times:

'Trane letting it rip
on the tenor sax,
the earth opening
with a great shudder,
a last spectacular spasm.

Millions of souls
ascending to Glory
like a jostling crowd
on a dime store escalator.

Uneasy seas,
darkness and foam,
rising to salute;
the precise Dürer moon
a pale sickle
rimmed with blood.

It's one hell of a party.

But Igneous Rock
is surprised to discover
that the word *yowzah!*
never actually appears
in the Bible.

IGNEOUS ROCK AND THE POLE DANCER

Apparently
pole dancers are not,
as he thought at first,
heir to an Eastern European
folk dancing tradition.

But some of these poor waifs
do seem to need saving—
or feeding, at the very least.

The Reverend Igneous Rock,
struggling to maintain an air
of dignified disgust, of honest outrage,
nevertheless finds himself embarrassed
to be seen in such a place as this
appalling den of iniquity.

The fires of Hell itself
will be as nothing
if Beulah ever finds out.

Igneous can truly say
(not that it will *help*)
that he entered the club
with the best intentions
on an errand of mercy—
having been told a young
sparrow of his flock,

whose parents are old friends
and whom he has known from infancy,
performs here nightly.

The child is nowhere in sight,
and the good Reverend suspects
he has been misinformed—
until he spies several prominent
members of the Board of Deacons
at the foot of the center stage
glancing his way and laughing.
Throbbing bass buries their words,
but he has gleaned the gist.

A pale girl strange to him
shimmies up the pole,
her taut body arced
in twitching light,
dark hair cascading
toward the floor.

On the velvet platform beneath her
greenbacks flutter like restless birds
stirred by indolent ceiling fans.
The whole thing's a ghoulish parody
of the Sunday morning collection.

Igneous is poleaxed.

He wants to call to her—
some righteous rebuke—
but lifting up his eyes
is suddenly struck speechless,

encountering an animal darkness
that will trouble his dreams
for many nights to come.

*—Thanks to Victor Buxbaum (1961–2013) for the "little
excursion" that inspired this poem.*

COLOPHON

In the back of his Bible
Igneous encounters the words
Text set in Dante.

He is uncertain
just how to take this.

THE REVEREND IGNEOUS ROCK PERUSES SHAKESPEARE'S SONNETS

Now here is poetry he *can* condone:
Not quite the Bible, but not bad at all—
Concise and poignant—rarely overblown—
With lines a man may easily recall.
His Beulah's eyes are "nothing like the sun,"
That's true enough; though surely they can burn.
He seriously doubts that anyone
Would ever call her "temperate," or discern
In her the beauty of a summer's day.
Her fulsome lips aren't rosy in the least,
Nor are her dusky cheeks. She's seldom "gay;"
Frankly, she often seems a perfect beast.
    Yet the good Reverend clearly recognizes
    Within these pages, how his own heart rises.

THE REVEREND IGNEOUS ROCK
PAYS A PASTORAL VISIT

Deep in the projects, rows of cinder block—
so military in aspect it won't do
to flatter them by calling them apartments—
stand rank on rank like barracks for the maimed
who gave their best in wars already lost.

The paint that scars these walls is dull and flat,
the uninspired pallor of stunned dust.
Damp laundry dripping from corroded railings
provides the only splash of hopeful color,
the only hint of vibrancy and life.

Across a gravely wounded parking lot,
into brown yards awash with stale sunlight,
striding among the rusted tricycles,
discarded lawn chairs, like an apparition,
comes the phenomenon that's Iggy Rock.

The Reverend of course is nattily attired
in a white linen suit that almost glows;
his panama hat's so intricate a weave
its bleached straw shimmers like the rarest silk;
a doubled sun brims in his mirrored shades.

He's keen to comfort a parishioner
down on his luck, though inwardly he wonders
what solace he can bring a frightened soul
here in the very bowels of despair

where everything smells of cigarettes and urine.

Still, this disciple's wise enough to know
the truest miracles are those we make
ourselves—or else, are brave enough to seek.
The guy seems genuinely glad to see him;
they share bad coffee laced with drugstore gin.

Though Igneous Rock is not a drinking man—
except in private, late, and secretly—
cheap booze ignites the wick of every nerve
until the rising warmth resembles grace,
a vice transmuted to a cautious blessing.

He takes the gnarled hand deformed by struggle
into his own, and meets the clouded eyes.
A voice destroyed by liquor and cocaine
thanks him for coming, sounding for a moment
like the hosanna of a shattered angel.

DOVES BLACKER THAN RAVENS

It's a scientific fact.
Doves and pigeons, if not precisely
the same species, are very closely related.
The Reverend Igneous Rock knows this.
But he's never really thought about it
until an elderly Latino neighbor—
not associated with his flock, the man's
devoutly Catholic—draws his attention
one morning to a rabble of filthy birds
foraging for crumbs along the curb.

All are dark, from a steely blue gray
inked with midnight like a Rorschach test,
to one or two uniformly black
as ravens—squabbling shadows
into which anemic sunlight falls
as into a ravenous maw in space.
There's no sign of the spotless silver dove
which his friend assures him
was a common sight on city streets
as recently as thirty years ago.

These grim beings are an omen to be heeded.
Misguided mayors and sanctimonious supervisors
committing genocide against the pigeons
in order to halt the spread of disease
are slowly siphoning the Holy Spirit.
And—the man warns Igneous gravely,
his wise eyes bright as mica

in his tanned and weathered face,
his waxed white mustache curling into light—
when the last pigeon dies, the world will end.

IGNEOUS ROCK IS GROWING OLDER

Never one to be cowed,
Igneous Rock approaches aging
the way he approaches unpleasant topics
in his sermons, clothing it
in language whose poetic pomposity
tries to disguise a disturbing truth.

He tells himself:

Youth ignites us; its sovereign fire
licks the soft wick of our bones:
a smoldering intensity, a coiled heat.

In later years the spirit cools;
flesh turns unyielding and rigid;
marrow incandesces to ash.

As for old age, he can't say yet.

But the signs Igneous has been given—
the world askew and dimming,
skies stirred like turgid water,
one false chord in every hymn—
are far from encouraging.

IGNEOUS ROCK'S DAY AT THE BEACH

"An ocean
That can't make up its mind."
—Cornelius Eady

Above the surging water
rises a sea of shoulders
blistered to crimson,
necks so angrily red
it hurts to look at them,
bald pates like the domed
arc of the pitiless sun.

Waves are edged with fierce light
that leaves its quivering script
lingering in back of the eye
long after one has turned away.

Waist-deep in the gush
of froth and kelp,
the Reverend Igneous Rock—
Jesus tee shirt plastered wetly
to his considerable torso,
for to be naked even now
would be most undignified—
wobbles into the onrushing tide.

Any pretense of solemnity
attending these proceedings
is seriously undercut
by the plastic inner tube

that engirths him—
a child's toy borrowed from Myrtle—
florescent pink with a horse's head,
eyes wide with astonishment,
that looks embarrassed to be there.

The good Reverend, alas,
has never learned to swim.

He studies the liquid horizon
dimming to mist in the distance,
reflecting on the scope of creation
and how, in the beginning,
the spirit of God must have
hovered over waters like these.

His meditations are cut short
by an enormous beach ball,
striped red and white like a flag,
which strikes him squarely in the face—
knocking him down
and sending him sputtering
beneath the surface.

God's glorious sea
leaves a foul taste in his mouth—
brine and the oil
of a century of passing freighters.

Stumbling back to shore
Igneous realizes
it's as if the ocean
can't make up its mind
whether to sing the grandly rolling

hosannas of the Lord
or drown itself and its song
in a putrid swirl of muck.

Maybe the world
can't make up
its mind either.

An Accident of Weather

❄

ABSURDITY FOR DRUM AND GLOCKENSPIEL

While I've never actually seen
the offending instrument,
I've heard it often enough:
the high, metallic stammer
of the glockenspiel, like the oddly
disturbing song of some solitary child,
wafting out of the JROTC room,
accompanied by a single faltering drum,
as I leave campus by a basement door
at the end of the school day.

This afternoon's no different,
save for the fact that something
vaguely familiar about this mutilated music
makes me pause a moment on the threshold,
searching my memory.

All at once I have it:
here is the transcendence
of "Jesu, Joy of Man's Desiring"—
more suited to fluted columns and stained glass—
reduced, in youthful hands,
to the merely mundane,
the melody earnestly stumbling
toward a Heaven that,
at the moment,
seems more remote than ever.

MOONFLOWERS

The morning glory's pale cousins,
they may grow to six inches across,
so blanched the blossoms resemble
immaculately folded napkins.

Gardeners warn against planting them
too close to windows, for the scent,
while sweet, can be cloying, and may
overpower the unwary.

All the manuals advise it's best
to allow them to grow near an arbor,
trellis, or fence that can support
the vining tendrils as they climb.

According to physics
the molecules in their petals
derive from the dust of exhausted stars,
beacons dead for millennia.

What we make of this knowledge
depends, I suppose, on circumstance.
Fortunes read in the skies nowadays
rely more on fusion than on fate.

On a damp winter morning, before dawn,
something ancient catches in the throats
of waking birds: a kernel of silence,
the aftertaste of some forgotten grief.

The light brimming on the horizon
is always the same pitiless light.
The moonflowers avert their gaze
from that terrible radiance.

OVID'S DUST

For a friend too afraid of being influenced.

Should Ovid's dust, reanimated, bloom
In the synaptic furrows of your brain,
There will be echoes. But do not assume
The work diminished; language is like rain
Scripting a passage on a windowpane;
The prosody's familiar, all the lines
Vernacular, both lucid and arcane;
Words swarm and spawn in intricate designs.
Frank admiration seldom undermines:
A pinch of Pynchon, dash of Dashiell Hammett,
Add spice and savor for the philistines.
Don't set aside your library, goddammit!
Although at first the going may be tough
Your own voice will prevail soon enough.

RESONANCE

The Stetson bought at Sheplers outside Denver
that winter before MaJe's cancer won
was to replace one given me by Victor—
who just a few years later would be dead,
killed in an accident near Santa Rosa—
which I could not retrieve after it was
swept from my head into the rainy dark.
Likewise the pocket watch procured on credit
although I didn't really have the money
will have to substitute for one that Pat
surprised me with not long before the tumor
sent dripping tendrils into her doomed brain:
with a discrete old world dignity,
it's elegant, yet lacks the resolute
conviction of the other, lost forever.
The Stetson too is finely wrought, although
the felt beneath my fingertips is not
as soft or supple as I might have wished.
These things are blameless in and of themselves,
but they lack *resonance*—a feathery,
an almost undetectable, "ghost weight,"
the residue of gracious lives cut short.

LISTENING FOR PLANES, 1917

My grandfather who fought
at Ypres said many years later
he'd memorized the whines
of aircraft engines overhead—
distinguishing Spad from Fokker,
distinctive pitches of friend and foe—
since to look up even for an instant
was to expose the pallor of flesh
beneath the dough boy helmet,
an open invitation to pilots
who still flew low enough
to aim a pistol or a bomb
with deadly accuracy.

THE WIDOWER CONSIDERS CANDLES

I miss those thin white saints
haloed in benign combustion,
their quiet, casual martyrdom,
wax feathering to wings, scenting
the night with a hint of the hive.

But I will not have them in this place:
they mimic the melancholy sheen
that settles on loss, the flames that took
your mortal body once you were gone,
dancing their mad, incandescent dance.

So there are none in my cupboards,
perhaps unfortunate, given that
ours is a time devoted to darkness,
the wick of the moon is at the window,
and dusk has been falling for years.

PICTURING SIXTO

And you can keep your symbols of success,
Then I'll pursue my own happiness.
　　　　　　　—S.R., "I'll Slip Away" (1973)

Sixto Rodriguez, I'm ashamed to admit
I'd never even heard of you
before I saw the documentary
Searching for Sugar Man,
your story too improbable to be true:
how two brilliant albums,
recorded in the early seventies,
sank without a trace in the States
but a bootleg somehow made its way
to apartheid South Africa,
was released and sold millions,
your anthemic folk songs a rallying cry
in the early days of the protests.

I bought both CDs and loved them,
but the scene from the film that haunts me
is not of you playing to enraptured crowds
in Cape Town upon your rediscovery,
laying to rest once and for all
rumors of a vaguely spectacular death.

Instead, I picture an ordinary gesture,
kneeling in the predawn gloom to light
a fire in an ashcan grate in the ramshackle house
where you've lived in downtown Detroit
for over forty years, leaving adulation behind,

returning to carpentry, demolition, and roofing,
living simply, as you always have.

AT 56

Love is not something I think about now,
like a yellowing Playbill folded in a book
misplaced on a high shelf, the performance
forgotten save for a hint of music,
delicate and strange, threaded through
some instrument I will never learn to play.

RELIQUARY

i.m.: Victor Leonard Buxbaum, 1961–2013

Somehow I know, even as it's happening,
that this is a dream. Beyond its borders,
in the waking world, you are still dead:
five months now. In the convoluted logic
of the dreamscape, I am living again
downtown in the apartment on Sutter,
somewhere I shouldn't reasonably be.
Although you were Jewish by birth,
Buddhist by inclination, you seem to
have attracted a sort of cult following,
old men in black, gaunt as priests,
who come knocking on my door,
their thin beards soft as spun sugar
in the hallway light. They want to
offer me a reliquary wherein repose
twisted metal fragments of the car
that ran you down, the shredded steel
still jeweled with your blood; they proffer
for my perusal icons in which your face
with its dark eyes and aquiline features
is the stylized visage of the Orthodox Christ,
like a specimen preserved in amber: calm,
conveying neither accusation nor forgiveness,
expressionless beneath a shroud of silence.

A MAGIC LANTERN SHOW

In an old video we showed,
one of my high school students
saw someone dialing a rotary phone
and asked what it was.
When I explained, she said,
"It looks hard!"

By now it's twenty years at least
since I heard the ephemeral
voice on a phone menu offer
"if you're calling from a rotary phone"
as a possible option.

Most of the adolescents I teach
can't read an analogue clock—
or decipher cursive, let alone write it.
One boy stood bewildered
before an electric typewriter,
no recognition on his face.

The world I knew is gradually fading,
like slides in cardboard frames,
relics of a pre-digital age,
that lose once-vivid colors
as they seep slowly into shadow.

And come to think of it,
those slides would themselves
have seemed strange

in my grandfather's time,
bastard offspring of what was then
a magic lantern show.

CUTTING THE DECK

I think abruptly of the yellow moss
that clogged the eyes of death's heads
in a colonial churchyard in Boston,
decades ago—

the names illegible now as healed scars—

the weathered headstones thin,
splayed like cards on a gray lawn,
save for a few
that had fallen to the weather,
face down so as not to tip their hand.

NOTHING HAPPENING, AT GREAT LENGTH

Poetry makes nothing happen.
—W. H. Auden

Heaped ranks of cumulus,
edged with a dull radiance,
move so slowly across
the monochromatic sky
that they seem frozen
on a photographic plate—
one of those heavy glass artifacts
on to which silver oxide gelatin
has seared the stillness
of the nineteenth century.

Unflinching, the lens has left us
fields on which the mounded
bones of the Mathew Brady dead,
whitened by wind and sun,
have begun—in the months
following the massacre—
to present a grisly visual echo
of the weather overhead.

This sky is the same sky
five generations later,
though the pliant green landscape
presses obliviously through the dust
of the long-ago-fallen.

All around us, nothing

is happening (as it will)
at great length. The march
of history plays to the muted
music of decay, like foxfire
which gnaws the dying world
into light—making of destruction
something gentle, even
oddly beautiful.

A HOMELESS MAN CITED FOR SLEEPING
IN THE MAIN LIBRARY

I dare not turn my head
to look: I dare not turn.

The voice that supplies
name and date of birth—
fully thirteen years
younger than I am—
has a timbre
like the sound
of glass being crushed.

Without seeing either,
I conjure clearly
the security guard
in his crisp blue uniform,
the wraith whose
pinched, unshaven face—
African, but hardly Black—
has faded to the pallor
of dirty parchment.

Cold light spills through high windows
on to them both—a ghastly radiance,
like the light implied in Dürer etchings.

AN ACCIDENT OF WEATHER

A.T. S., Oberlin, Fall 1977

Try, if you must, to persuade me
that this street so slick the asphalt
shouldering the morning mist
shines as it might after rain,

this street where a cataract sky
is mirrored, featureless
as though it secreted some meaning
beyond an accident of weather,

cannot possibly lead us to any future
save for the one that you foresee.

I will listen to what you tell me
without speaking, perspiration chill
on my face in the breaking dawn.
I will contradict nothing.

And when you've said your piece
and turn to go, I will study the way
your footprints linger an instant
on a film of oily moisture
before they disappear, healing
behind your retreat like wounds.

RICE BALLS

Rice balls wrapped in aluminum foil:
that's the image that keeps turning up.
Sultan School, Honolulu, 1961.
A classmate who wore a steel helmet
to protect the place where the plates
of his skull hadn't closed,
leaving his brain vulnerable
beneath a thin sheath of hair, skin,
and flesh. The way his eyes
rolled uneasily in orbits of their own
as though perpetually fixed
on something no one else could see.
How his delicate, tea-colored hands,
so clumsy on the playground
with a ball, deftly manipulated
chopsticks with a dexterity
I cannot manage even today.
The silence that seemed sewn
onto lips from which no words
ever issued, busy as they were
with the simple, primal act of eating;
the quietly graceful dance of rice;
the sticks from which not one
grain ever fell.

BEGINNING THE STORY

The way moonlight tumbles through
a glass of whiskey in a darkened room
is perhaps a suitable starting point.
But it is not enough. We require as well
an open window, a bitten moon,
a raven so large the wires
sag beneath its weight, an enigma
with eyes like shards of glass.
If the night is starless, so much the better;
one cannot, however, attach much
importance to omens. An ivory letter
opener from another century, ornately
carved, lies on a blotter near the whiskey,
pale against paper stained
by the dimness of this world.
A letter opener hungry for news
of some place from which no word
has come for a long time.

OMENS

Omens were certainly present,
if not in Tarot or dark scrawls of tea leaves,
then on seismographs, thermometers,
between the lines in the pages of newspapers.

Heavy rains pummeled the Rockies,
transforming prairies at their base
into a flood plains whose waters mirrored
skies the sickly color of sodden clay.

Late that summer, Yosemite burned;
smoke black with the heaviness of sap
drifted over its reservoir;
tap water as far away as San Francisco
tasted for weeks afterward of ashes.

Charlatan preachers blamed End Times,
citing chapter and verse, although it may
after all have been only smog that made
the moon appear to weep tears of blood.

In early autumn, along the coast,
weather unseasonably warm,
light beat hills to burnished copper;
wine that year was a fine vintage, full and rich;
lovers strolled through long blue twilights,
wished on stars of unsurpassed brightness.

SHE'S NOT THERE

Taking the stage at Stern Grove:
the Zombies, not the somnambulant corpses
that dominate movies and television these days,
but the iconic British rock group,
graying and crinkled but still vibrant,
Colin Blunstone's creepy tenor
soaring over a rumbling bass.

On the sides of the ravine, under the trees,
the crowd, all tee shirts and sunscreen,
applauds old favorites: "Tell Her No,"
"Time of the Season." The air's dense, hot,
the medicinal treacle of eucalyptus
battling the cloying of cannabis.

For a moment, it's possible to imagine
the Summer of Love risen from its flowery grave,
and I wonder who was playing here then.

But the illusion lingers only briefly,
dissipating like a vaguely pleasant dream.
Years sift through slanting light like pollen,
like the husks of last season's seeds.

She's not there? None of us are.

THE FORGOTTEN BEES

In warmer weather, bees would make frenzied
music in these bushes stripped gaunt and bare
against the brown and ruined lawns of winter,
although this year they are not clothed in snow.

Bees! City boy, I barely remember them:
one of so many once-commonplace things
taken for granted in childhood, then misplaced
beneath the dull accumulation of the years.

If I had come in summer, the surrounding peaks
glittering sternly with ice would instead be vibrant
with that season, nearly hidden by abundant foliage;
the air green and fragrant with freshly cut grass.

And the bees—the forgotten bees—would dart
like flecks of light among indolent blossoms,
single-minded in their pursuit of sweetness,
surer of satiety than I am of anything now.

RUTABAGAS

My grandfather, Clarence Smith, Sr.,
returned home from the Great War
to load his seed drill with sweet corn
that was spit into the furrowed earth
as rapidly as rounds from a Browning—
and every so often he varied the mix
with rutabaga seeds that slumbered
beneath the slim green cornstalks
until late in the season, after harvest,
when my father, still a boy, would
rummage through the scarred fields
in search of their belated bounty.

YEATS AND THE COCKROACH

Dust jacket photos, 1933,
Show us a man no doubt already old:
Shadows around his eyes have pooled deeply,
The light disclosing him is thin and cold.
Again, I'm moving. Cardboard boxes brim
With poetry, novels, essays, plays, and speeches;
Out in broad daylight, disrespecting him,
An arrogant cockroach navigates his features.
The poet William Yeats has come to this:
Once Ireland hurt him into poetry,
And now this lowliest of creatures is
Twitching its way across his memory:
A mindless flake the color of thick rust
That will abide when poems turn to dust.

IN MEMORY OF SEAMUS HEANEY

Died August 30, 2013

You left us in diminishing summer:
the brooks vigorous, swollen and full-throated,
airports thronged with homeward-wending tourists,
foliage, in Dublin and Derry, just goldening to rust;
left us on an otherwise unremarkable day, in mild weather,
when heat rose in soft tatters from murmuring pavements.

In this age when immortality seems assured us all,
if only in cyberspace where the faces of the dead
linger forever, unchanging, pixelated and luminous,
a few thousand, perhaps, will remember this day,
bookmark an obituary, modify a timeline on Facebook.

You were modest and approachable, the papers tell us:
endured with grace and dignity the packed public readings,
journalists, earnest undergraduates seeking approbation.
Beneath it all lay Ireland's plain-spoken rural diction,
from which you excavated layers of meaning
like a farmhand digging peat, the ground below
smoky with ancient bones.

PULP FICTION

Vodka Martini had always hated her name. Some sense of humor her parents must have had, the lushes; it made her job as a cocktail waitress seem somehow inevitable, like a rap sheet, a good dose of the clap. And in a dive like this, no less. Fly specks riddled the mirror behind the bar, wounding the reflection of the whiskey, beyond which brooded a gray and anonymous city whose skies seemed always bloated with the threat of rain. Then there was Joe, down at the far end, polishing the taps with an air of sullen disinterest. *Joe!* Bald and shriveled, the man was a walking cliché. As she made eye contact, he smiled bitterly, his features heavy with boredom. Few customers made demands on them at that hour, since it was well past two in the morning. An old drunk in a corner booth scrutinized a half-empty pint as though it were a chalice brimming with sad, holy light. A gaggle of washed-up hookers—regulars—chatted at a table in the rear, the holes in their fishnet stockings visible even from where she stood, their knobby knees bloodied by the stuttering neon above La Puce Ivre, the flophouse across the street. It was a Tuesday, and nothing ever happened on Tuesday, as Vodka knew. But just then, the door flew open, banging against the ancient Wurlitzer which, abruptly lighting, halfheartedly began a sentimental old ballad. The door flew open, and everything changed. A tall, lanky figure stood in the doorway, silhouetted against the endless drizzle. "Snowden Shovel!," Vodka gasped. The same crushed-ice voice, same wry, world-weary grin. "Hello, Angel. It's been a long time."

JOHN CLARE IN THE MADHOUSE

I am the self-consumer of my woes,
They rise and vanish in oblivious host. . .
—John Clare, 1793-1864; "I Am"

I am less than a shadow, less than a glimmer of starlight.
I wonder in Whose name distant galaxies throb like blisters.
I hear weak winter sunlight stumbling earthward.
I see the festering air: nearly opaque, grown heavy
    as blown glass.
I want these troubled longings—O my lost Mary!—to cease.

I am less than a shadow, less than a glimmer of starlight.
I pretend these damaged verses will not die unspoken.
I feel nothing, bury the burdensome beat of my heart.
I touch a memory, and it falls instantly to dust.
I worry the bones of my hands, worn smooth as dice.
I cry for verdant fields, the beauty of a dead crow
    swarming with flies.

I am less than a shadow, less than a glimmer of starlight.
I understand less and less with every haunted sunrise.
I parrot shards of a dead tongue
    that wound my lips like prayers.
I dream in terrible colors never imagined before.
I try nothing at which I haven't already failed.
I hope only rarely, for trifles, and never for long.
I am less than a shadow, less than a glimmer of starlight.

GREEN GROW THE RUSHES, O

As for instance in the gutters
along the sloping tar paper roofs
of barracks on Treasure Island,
abandoned structures empty
perhaps since World War Two,
where nature has marshaled
brigades of pale shoots
that flicker like soft green fire
in the evening breeze, ignited
by the sun just now sinking
seaward behind the headlands,
turning to silhouette the towers
of the Golden Gate Bridge.

NOCTURNE FOR MOONLIGHT
AND PHONOGRAPH

In a darkened room far back in time,
someone puts on a phonograph record

of the sound of a summer thunderstorm,
although the weather tonight is clear;

the hiss and crackle in the grooves
hints at a strange electricity in the air.

Outside it is April, a year no one will remember;
perhaps a nearby river is in flood, perhaps not.

Shoots impale the crushed black earth,
tongues in consultation with the wind.

Elms like crones lean closer, listening,
grizzled with the light of a taciturn moon.

WORLDS BEYOND THE VISIBLE

And if I don't know by now
that you are gone, when will I learn?
                    —*Marsha Campbell*

Nature's relentlessness
can be irritating at times
like this, when it's simply
too beautiful to stay inside:
the morning cloudless, warm;
the glissandi of birds;
eucalyptus scenting
the air like a lozenge.

It's Sunday, of course,
a day I've learned to dread
because of the oppressive
weight of its silences.
I stumble through sunlight,
breeze sharp against my skin,
worlds beyond the visible
pressing in on every side.

On Irving, people are out;
shops and bars are open.
If grief has insinuated itself
anywhere into this scene,
it is the verdigris that clings
to old church bells, as the chimes
of St. Anne of the Sunset,
obdurate in their optimism,
clamor to the sky.

Index of Titles

ABOUT THE AUTHOR

ROBERT LAVETT SMITH lives in San Francisco. He holds a B.A in French from Oberlin College, where he also studied creative writing with Stuart Friebert and David Young, and an M.A. in English from the University of New Hampshire, studying with Charles Simic and Mekeel McBride. After graduating from UNH, he joined the Master Class at the 92nd Street YMCA in New York City, where he studied with Galway Kinnell. In addition to *The Widower Considers Candles*, he has authored four small-press chapbooks and two previous full-length efforts, *Everything Moves With A Disfigured Grace* and *Smoke In Cold Weather: A Gathering of Sonnets*.

A NOTE ON THE FONTS

This book is set in High Tower Text, designed by American type designer Tobias Frere-Jones in 1996 and based on Nicolas Jensen's 1470 Venetian roman. Titles are set in Gotham Black, one of a family of geometric sans-serif digital typefaces modeled on New York City street signs and designed by Frere-Jones in 2000.

www.ingramcontent.com/pod-product-compliance
Lightning Source LLC
Chambersburg PA
CBHW020853090426
42736CB00008B/359